QUEEN'S OWN HIGHLANDERS

Also by Trevor Royle in the same series

The Royal Scots
The Black Watch
The Royal Highland Fusiliers

QUEEN'S OWN HIGHLANDERS

A Concise History

TREVOR ROYLE

MAINSTREAM
PUBLISHING

EDINBURGH AND LONDON

First published in Great Britain in 2007 by
MAINSTREAM PUBLISHING COMPANY
(EDINBURGH) LTD
7 Albany Street
Edinburgh EH1 3UG

ISBN 9781845960926

A catalogue record for this book is available
from the British Library

Typeset in Bembo

Printed in Great Britain by
William Clowes Ltd, Beccles, Suffolk

Contents

Preface

The Queen's Own Highlanders has a relatively short record of service but through its two antecedent regiments – The Seaforth Highlanders and Queen's Own Cameron Highlanders – its history and traditions reach back into the late eighteenth century, when the government of the day raised Highland regiments for service in India and North America. Its recent history also reflects the changes that have taken place in the country's defence policies in the years following the Second World War. In 1961, as a result of the need to reduce the army's infantry regiments by amalgamating 30 infantry battalions, The Seaforth Highlanders and Queen's Own Cameron Highlanders combined to form Queen's Own Highlanders. More than 30 years later there was a greater change when the regiment was amalgamated with The Gordon Highlanders to form The Highlanders (Seaforth, Gordons and Camerons). It, too, was short-lived and emerged with a new identity. In March 2006 The Royal Regiment of Scotland came into being with five regular battalions, one of which was The Highlanders, 4th battalion The Royal Regiment of Scotland. Inevitably the changes created a great deal of sadness in the army community and more widely throughout Scotland, with regret being expressed for the loss of some cherished names and the conversion of regiments into a new formation. However, the history of the British Army shows that the story of its regiments has been one of constant development, with cutbacks, amalgamations and changes of name being part of a process of evolution stretching back over several centuries. In every case the development has not led to a diminution of the army's capabilities but has produced new regiments which are the equal of their predecessors.

Together with the other books in the series this concise history has been written to mark this latest transformation in Scottish and British military history. It is not a new regimental history of the regiment and its predecessors, but I hope it will be a useful addition to the regiment's historiography. Invariably, as is the case with the other concise regimental histories, it also reflects the history of the British Army and the empire in which it served. I owe a tremendous debt to previous regimental historians, whose books are listed in the bibliography. It goes without saying, I hope, that the history of the regiment could not have been attempted without a thorough reading of the existing regimental histories and records, and anyone familiar with the regiment will recognise the debt I owe to Lieutenant-Colonel Angus Fairrie's encyclopaedic account of the regiment. Illustrations are reproduced by kind permission of The Highlanders Museum Trustees.

For help throughout the project I would like to thank everyone at Home Headquarters, The Highlanders, Cameron Barracks, Inverness, especially the Regimental Secretary until 2006, Lieutenant-Colonel Alastair Cumming. At Fort George, the home of the Queen's Own Highlanders' museum, I received unstinting help with the illustrations from Colonel George Latham and Lieutenant-Colonel Angus Fairrie. Grateful thanks

PREFACE

are also due to Brigadier Hughie Monro, who gave his blessing to the project during his period of office as Colonel of The Highlanders.

Trevor Royle

CHAPTER ONE

Beginnings

The Queen's Own Highlanders was formed in 1961 as a result of the amalgamation of two of Scotland's most famous Highland infantry regiments, The Seaforth Highlanders and Queen's Own Cameron Highlanders. Their antecedent regiments, 72nd, 78th and 79th Highlanders were raised at the end of the eighteenth century as part of the British government's policy of recruiting Highland soldiers into the British Army to serve in the wars against France and their founders belonged to two of the most influential families in the Highlands and Western Islands of Scotland, Mackenzie of Seaforth and Cameron of Erracht. Both regiments owed their existence, too, to the events that followed the defeat of the Jacobite army at Culloden in 1746 and to the subsequent subjugation of the Highlands and the despoliation of its Gaelic culture. The destruction of Highland military power and the Clearances of the traditional clan lands were the beginning of the end of a way of life which was barely understood by outsiders, not least Lowland Scots, but it has to be said that, at the time, the process was largely welcomed. In the aftermath of the union of the parliaments in 1707 and the economic benefits of 'heavenly Hanoverianism' it was thought no bad thing to have this lawless area with its savage population and heathen way of life (for so it seemed) brought under control. What to do with the Highlanders was another matter. Either they could accept modernity and the union, or they could be moved elsewhere to make new lives, courtesy of landowners who regarded themselves not as destroyers but as liberal reformers. As for the soldierly instincts of their tenants, these could be offered to the British Army at a time when it was being used as an imperial gendarmerie to expand the country's growing colonial holdings.

In fact, steps had already been taken to channel Highland militarism into the service of the state with the creation of the Independent Companies of the Highland Watch in 1739. These paramilitary units had been brought into being earlier in the century as independent companies to control the approaches to the Highlands to prevent smuggling and generally to help keep the peace in the area where the Lowlands gave way to the Highlands. They had been a mixed success, being irregular forces with a poor command structure, and the creation of this new unit under the command of the Earl of Crawford represented a breakthrough in that it was given a number, 43rd (later 42nd), and placed in the British Army's order of battle. Later it was better known as The Black Watch or Royal Highland Regiment. But it was during the Seven Years War that the prime minister, William Pitt the Elder, acting on a suggestion made by King George II, opened the door for the creation of the Highland regiments. Highlanders were regarded as good soldiers, their powers of endurance and fighting qualities had become evident during the earlier Jacobite rebellions. Here was a ready supply of soldiers who would do their duty, and their clan loyalties would bring a sense of coherence and reliability which would translate into good military practice. As the days of the clan system were numbered after Culloden and would soon disappear, other than as a sentimental entity based on chiefdoms, tartan and yearning for a lost past, the Highland regiments became handy substitutes.

Not that their creation was universally popular, either in England or in Scotland. Memories of Highland violence and savagery were still vivid, but Pitt argued that the recruitment of the Highlanders served two purposes — a steady supply of good soldiers for service in Europe, North America and India, and a means of finally pacifying a previously troublesome area by ridding it of its warlike young men. If they were killed in the process, then that might be no bad thing either: it was clear that many Highlanders would not return to their native lands, especially if they were fighting in colonial wars. And if the policy of raising the regiments was intended to further the depopulation of the Highlands, the fighting in America certainly helped the process. Once disbanded, many Highland soldiers settled in America, where it was hoped they would provide a loyal bulwark against any secession movement. Within the space of 20 years rebel Highlanders had been transmogrified into loyal patriots. In 1766 Pitt defended in parliament his decision to raise the Scottish regiments:

> I have no local attachments: it is indifferent to me, whether a man was rocked in his cradle on this side or that of the Tweed. I sought for merit wherever it was to be found. It is my boast that I was the first minister who looked for it, and I found it in the mountains of the north. I called it forth, and drew it into your service, a hardy and intrepid race of men! Men who, when left by your jealousy became prey to the artifices of your enemies and had gone nigh to have overturned the state, in the war before last. These men, in the last war were brought to combat on your side: they served with fidelity, as they fought with valour, and conquered for you in every part of the world: detested

be the national reflections against them! They are unjust, groundless, illiberal, unmanly!

How did this work out in practice? To a great extent the figures speak for themselves. Between 1714 and 1763 a quarter of the officers serving in the British Army were Scots, proportionally more than the English. Of 208 officers who were also members of parliament from 1750 to 1794, 56 were Scots. At the same time, one in four regimental officers were Scots and Scots were used to receiving high command while fighting in the European and colonial wars waged by Britain throughout the eighteenth century. Between 1725 and 1800 no fewer than 37 Highland regiments were raised to serve in the British Army, and by the end of the period the numbers involved are estimated at 70,000 men.

From the very outset the territorial links of the regiments were vital, not just for recruiting but also for maintaining group cohesion and loyalty. The system had other benefits. Landowners who had supported the Jacobites were able to demonstrate their loyalty by raising regiments as a quid pro quo. Most considered themselves to be Highland gentlemen and if estates had been forfeited, the raising of a regiment was a useful means of retrieving family honour and making good lost ground. That was an important consideration, as the creation of a regiment depended on social status and financial capacity, the going rate for raising and equipping a regiment being £15,000, an enormous sum (nearly £1.5 million today) considering that the average annual pay for a private soldier was £18. A landowner wishing to raise a regiment had to have contacts at the highest social level, as it was the king who gave authority for the regiment to be raised in his name. The actual commission for the commanding officer was signed by the Secretary for War but at the time the final arbiter was King George II.

Once the order and warrant had been issued the regiment

came into being and the commanding officer set about recruiting. For the senior officers, a regimental commander would look to his closest family and friends and they in turn helped to recruit the soldiers from the tenants on their estates. When Kenneth Mackenzie, the Earl of Seaforth, raised the 78th (later 72nd) Highlanders in 1778, half of the soldiers came from his own estates while the rest were recruited from Mackenzie lands in Wester Ross. To make up numbers it was common practice to take on English and Irish soldiers. Blandishments included the promise of booty and plunder from campaigns overseas, India being regarded as a treasure trove, and alcohol also came into play. To get some idea of how the system worked there is the well-attested example of the raising of the 79th Highlanders by Alan Cameron of Erracht in 1793. He was not a rich man and did not enjoy the support of a large estate yet a combination of patriotism and the chance to make a fortune abroad encouraged him to raise his regiment of Highlanders. He had to work hard at it for not only was recruitment a problem but he also had to face the opposition of his own family. Fortunately Cameron of Erracht enjoyed widespread respect and according to local records in the Lochaber district the 79th was raised 'on the sheer strength of his personal popularity . . . he was a king of men in personal appearance and large-hearted and liberal handed and in their estimation an ideal Highlander'. This was an important consideration – not only did Alan Cameron enjoy the respect of his men but, as a contemporary Gaelic poem written by John MacCodrum makes clear, the regiment was bound together by bonds of clan loyalty:

> You raised a regiment from a band of merry active men, lads smart in their dress, agile, even-tempered and unerring, steadfast young men and hardy. On every occasion they shall overcome, their lead shot shall be buzzing, swift

to good effect . . . the well-disciplined officers all well educated, Clan Maclean of the banners with you and the Company of Lochy at full speed, hearty heroes of Clan Donald, generous, boisterous and aggressive . . . this is the stout regiment that shall be renowned for achievements.

And indeed they were. The Cameron Highlanders quickly built up a solid reputation fighting under the Duke of York in the Netherlands and under Wellington in the Peninsula and Waterloo campaigns. The other Highland regiments gave equally loyal and valiant service, and being allowed to wear tartan they had become an easily identified section of the British Army, so different from the other line-infantry regiments with their standard-issue red coats. With the allure of their uniforms, Scottish soldiers became an instantly recognised and widely feared element of the British Army and their service in Africa, India and North America helped to consolidate Britain's growing mercantile empire.

78TH (LATER 72ND) HIGHLANDERS

In 1778 Kenneth Mackenzie, Earl of Seaforth, offered to raise a regiment of Highland soldiers at a time when the war in North America was going badly – three years earlier the colonists had started a revolt against British rule – and recruiting was proving to be extremely difficult. A Letter of Service was produced on 8 January 1778 and four months later 47 officers and 1,082 soldiers were recruited into the 78th Highland Foot which was passed fit for service at Elgin and moved south, first to Aberdeen and then to Edinburgh. However, not all was well within the ranks of the new regiment. Most of the men owed their loyalty to Mackenzie and they were proud Highlanders who did not respect the rigours of contemporary military discipline. In no small measure they considered themselves to be gentlemen, and were unused to being treated otherwise. Their pride was further dented by the absence of the promised engagement bounties, and the last straw was provided by a rumour that they had been engaged by the East India Company and would be sent to India instead of the American colonies. In fact the regiment was bound for the Channel Islands to replace Lord MacLeod's 73rd (later 71st) Highlanders but the damage had been done and the arrival at Leith of five troop transports seemed to confirm the rumour. When the 78th paraded outside the castle on 22 September the unthinkable happened. Led by a group of Macraes from Kintail around 400 soldiers broke ranks and marched off behind a piper down the Canongate before wheeling north to reach the shore of the Forth estuary. Seaforth and the rump of the regiment pursued them and there was a brief and somewhat ludicrous altercation before the mutineers retired back towards Arthur's Seat while the loyal members of the regiment were hastily put aboard the waiting transports in the roads of Leith.

It was a tense situation. The 'Wild Macraes' (as they had been dubbed) were in a strong position at the top of Arthur's Seat and at first refused all attempts to parley. Cavalry was called out to surround the area but fortunately the senior officer in Scotland, Lieutenant-General Sir James Oughton, was determined to avoid bloodshed. Not only did he understand the depth of feeling that had provoked the mutiny but he was also aware that the soldiers' action enjoyed widespread support – a correspondent in the *Aberdeen Journal* compared the mutineers on Arthur's Seat to 'the warriors of Ossian, seen from afar, with their glittering arms on the tops of mountains'. From a professional view Oughton could not afford to lose an entire infantry regiment and although it went against the grain he agreed to accept the mutineers' demands. The bounties would be paid, a promise was given that the 78th would not be posted to India and free pardons were granted to all. A subsequent Court of Inquiry papered over the cracks and, suitably mollified, the mutineers marched down to Leith to embark on the transports which took them to the Channel Islands.

Their first duty was to guard the islands against French invasion, as France had declared war on Britain to support the rebellious colonists during the fighting in North America. In April 1779 the regiment took part in its first engagement when it repelled an attempted French landing and two years later it was also involved in the Battle of Jersey when a stronger French force of 700, led by Baron de Rollecourt, succeeded in landing on Jersey and occupied the capital, St Helier. Five companies of the 78th took part in the operations to dislodge the French and the danger was averted. In contradiction to the promises made in Edinburgh the 78th embarked for service in India and it proved to be a miserable experience. The voyage lasted ten months and by the time the 78th reached Madras (now Chennai), 250 men had succumbed to sickness and disease. Amongst them was the commanding officer, the Earl of Seaforth, who died of fever off the coast of West Africa. He was succeeded by his second cousin, Thomas Mackenzie-Humberston, who had taken his mother's name when he succeeded to her estates in Lincolnshire. Later he himself succeeded, albeit briefly, to the Seaforth earldom.

Once ashore, the regiment had to accustom itself to the heat and exchanged kilts and belted plaids of black and green government tartan for white linen trousers. They were soon in action, fighting in the service of the East India Company in the war against Tipu, the Sultan of Mysore, the son of Hyder Ali.

Throughout the eighteenth century India, like North America, provided a battleground for rival French and British interests as each country tried to consolidate commercial supremacy on the ruins of the Mogul Empire. Although the French had lost heavily as a result of the Seven Years War – in 1757 Robert Clive's victory at Plassey secured Bengal for Britain

– the fighting in India opened opportunities for them to support rulers who were opposed to the British presence. In 1780 British authority was confined to Bengal and the coastal strips around Madras and Bombay; they also propped up Mohammed Ali, also known as the Nawab Walajah, the ruler of the Carnatic (the hinterland of Madras) but his authority was under constant threat from Hyder Ali, the ruler of neighbouring Mysore. Not only had Hyder Ali proved that he possessed a sound military mind during the First Mysore War of 1767–69, fought against the British after he had usurped power in Mysore, but his army had been reinforced by French officers and was equipped with French artillery. The 78th was in action in June 1783 to secure the port of Cuddalore after it had been captured by French forces; it also took part in the operations against Tipu's fort at Palghautcherry before the fighting in the Carnatic was brought to an end by the Treaty of Paris, which concluded the war in North America.

The coming of peace also brought an end to the reason for the 78th's existence. Its men had enlisted for 'three years or until the end of the Rebellion' and now they were entitled to be discharged. The only alternative was to soldier on in return for a new bounty of ten guineas, and some 300 of Seaforth's Highlanders agreed to remain in India in their regiment's uniform. For the rest there was the long journey home. As John Prebble put it in his history of mutinies in Highland regiments, for them it was an awesome experience: 'Ten thousand sea-miles from their cool blue Highlands, with little money and speaking Gaelic only for the most part, it is astonishing that any of the disbanded men found their way home.' One more change awaited the men who stayed behind in India. Three years later, when the size of the infantry was reduced to 77 regiments, Seaforth's regiment was renumbered 72nd and in that guise it took part in the next phase of the fighting against Tipu Sultan (as he had become). At the time of the renumbering the regiment's strength was 29 officers and 934 men. This was a quiet period for the regiment and it was brought to an end in 1790 when Tipu Sultan invaded the province of Travancore, which was in alliance with the East India Company. A field army was created under the command of Major-General Sir William Medows, an experienced soldier whose plan was to gain possession of the province of Coimbatore before invading Mysore from the south. The 72nd formed part of the left wing of the force in company with the 71st Highlanders (later 1st Highland Light Infantry). Coimbatore was occupied quickly and efficiently but Medows' move failed to tempt Tipu into a fixed battle. At the end of the year Medows' army joined forces at Darampore with a force from Bengal.

Command of the army now passed to the Earl Cornwallis, governor-general of India, who had become impatient at the lack of action in southern India and the failure to deal with Tipu Sultan. By the beginning of March 1791 Cornwallis had taken his army to Kolar, within two days' marching of Bangalore, which was then put under siege. Cornwallis's next objective was Seringapatam, Tipu's capital, which was reached on 13 May but, finding it heavily fortified, he was forced to order a withdrawal to Bangalore where he decided to set about the destruction of the hill forts in the immediate vicinity. The reduction of these strongpoints by the end of the year permitted Cornwallis to return to Seringapatam, a heavily fortified town on an island between two branches of the River Cauvery.

It was a formidable target and although Cornwallis knew that he had to bring his men to battle he was by no means certain that he would be able to reduce such a heavily defended fortress. His plan was to attack the enemy in three divisions, the left and right wings attacking on the flanks while the centre, under his personal command, would attack into the heart of Tipu's army and attempt to cross over to the island. This division was composed of four

British regiments, 52nd (Oxfordshire) Foot and the 71st, 72nd and 74th Highlanders supported by three battalions of the army of the East India Company. As described by Lieutenant (later Lieutenant-Colonel) Ronald Campbell in his journal (quoted in Cannon's *Records of the 72nd*), it was a confused close-quarter battle as the infantrymen struggled to cross the river, waist deep in the swirling waters, and then to engage the enemy:

> We rushed among them, and those who did not save themselves by immediate flight, were shot or bayoneted. The greatest number of them ran down to the Carriagat pagoda, where they made a stand and kept up a sharp fire until we were almost close to them; then retired under our fire to the foot of the hill, where they were joined by a strong body from the plain, and made a stand by a small choultry [colonnade], from which a flight of steps led to the bridge across the nulla [water-course]. By this time the general attack on the enemy's lines had commenced, and there was an almost connected sheet of fire from right to left; musketry, guns and rockets rending the air with their contending noise.

The fighting continued until dawn on 8 February 1792 when Cornwallis's men woke to find that Tipu Sultan's army had removed itself into the safety of Seringapatam, leaving the island in their hands. The resulting siege lasted a month before Tipu sued for terms. As a reward for the services of the British regiments each private soldier in the 72nd received a bounty of £14 from the East India Company, a tidy sum which was not much less than a year's wages. Their losses were one officer and 14 soldiers killed and four officers and 43 soldiers wounded or missing.

The outbreak of war with revolutionary France in February

1793 gave the 72nd further opportunities for action, taking part in the siege of the French fort at Pondicherry. Although an attack on Mauritius was abandoned the following year, the annexation by France of Holland in 1795 meant that all Dutch colonies in the area were taken over by the British as a precautionary measure. In August the 72nd was part of an invasion force which landed in Ceylon (now Sri Lanka) and captured the fortresses of Trincomalee and Batticaloa. In 1798 the 72nd returned home after 17 years of service in India and immediately started recruiting at its depot in Perth. Its Highland uniform was restored but manpower shortages and competition from other regiments hampered recruiting, with the result that the new century began with the 72nd's strength a miserly 214 officers and men. Two things saved the regiment: to counter the recruitment crisis the government passed legislation which allowed men from the fencible forces, formed for home defence, to transfer to line-infantry regiments, and the 72nd transferred to Ireland, which was always a ready source of recruits for the British Army. During its deployment in that country between 1800 and 1805 the regiment was gradually brought up to full strength. The regimental records for the period between 1808 and 1822 provide a telling assessment of the numbers of recruits and their national backgrounds: 2,022 Scots, 397 English, 526 Irish, 90 foreign (principally from the German states with a small number of Caribbeans in the band). Curiously, a significant number of recruits came from the east coast county of Angus.

78TH HIGHLANDERS

In 1793 Britain entered into 22 years of war against revolutionary France with a small, ill-equipped and demoralised army which had to take on an enemy whose armed forces numbered half a million. Years of cutbacks and inefficiency had left Britain with an army which Lord Macaulay described in his *History of England* as 'the laughing stock of all Europe', and in the opening rounds of the war against the French matters did not improve with a series of disasters in Europe and some half-hearted exploits in the West Indies:

> It could not boast one single brilliant exploit. It had never shown itself on the Continent but to be beaten, chased, forced to re-embark, or forced to capitulate. To take some sugar islands in the West Indies, to scatter some mob of half-naked Irish peasants, such were the most splendid victories won by the British troops under Pitt's auspices.

Having cut back the size of the army in the wake of the loss of the American colonies, steps had to be taken to raise new regiments and later, in 1804, to add additional battalions to existing regiments. Against that background Francis Humberston Mackenzie of Seaforth, brother of Thomas who had died in Bombay in 1783 and whom he succeeded as chief of the Clan Mackenzie, petitioned the government to raise a regiment of Highlanders. On 7 March 1793 he received a Letter of Service and by coincidence the new regiment was numbered 78th; once again the majority came from the Mackenzies' own lands and a contemporary regimental record describes them in glowing terms:

> This was an excellent body of men, healthy, vigorous and efficient; attached and obedient to their officers, temperate and regular; in short, possessing those principles of integrity and moral conduct which constitute a valuable soldier. The duty of officers was easy with such men, who only required to be told what duty was expected of them. A young officer endowed with sufficient judgement to direct them in the field, possessing energy and spirit to ensure the respect and confidence of soldiers and prepared on every occasion *to*

show them the eye of the enemy, need not desire a command
that would sooner and more permanently establish his
professional character, if employed on an active campaign,
than that of 1000 such men as composed this regiment.

The new regiment wore the government or Black Watch tartan
overlaid with red and white stripes and the red coatee had buff
facings. Buff jackets were worn by the bandsmen, who also wore the
Royal Stuart tartan. In August the 78th was ready for active service
and, like its Seaforth predecessor, moved south to the Channel
Islands where it formed the garrison on Guernsey. Meanwhile a
second battalion was raised in 1794 and from its facings was known
as the Ross-shire Buffs, a name that was incorporated into the
regiment's title the following year. The deployment in Guernsey
was a prelude to the 78th's first posting overseas, when the 1st
battalion formed part of an expeditionary force of British and
Hessian regiments commanded by the Duke of York, King George
III's second son, which was despatched to Flanders to support the
Austrian army fighting against the French. Although they and the
other British regiments gave a good account of themselves under
difficult circumstances, they were outnumbered three to one by the
French army under the command of General Jean Houchard and
at one stage the British force was obliged to abandon its artillery. A
series of exhausting marches and counter-marches dominated the
campaign which was memorialised in the children's nursery song
'The Grand Old Duke of York' and following the surrender of
Brussels and Antwerp to the French in April 1795 the remnants of
York's army were forced to withdraw to Britain after making their
way to Bremerhaven.

During the operations the 78th first saw action in October,
near the village of Rossem in the Bommeler-Waart, where it lost its
first casualties to fire from its Dutch allies. At the end of the month

the regiment moved to the Duke of York's headquarters near Arnhem and, following a night march towards Nijmegen, engaged French forces with the bayonet. Towards the end of the month the regiment was brigaded with 12th (later The Suffolk Regiment), 33rd (later 1st Duke of Wellington's Regiment) and 42nd (later 1st Black Watch), and with them they took part in the fighting along the River Waal, which had frozen over due to the extreme coldness of the winter weather. The fighting continued for 48 hours but the arrival of French reinforcements forced the British formations to retreat towards the village of Geldermalsen, where the regiments formed picquets to cover the retreat of the main force. By then the French had superior numbers and attacked the village with cavalry, a move which prompted the British to use two artillery pieces to protect them as they attempted to fall back. The 78th was in the advance supported by the 42nd when they were attacked by French cavalry and lost four men killed and seven wounded during the fighting, which saw the Highlanders firing an average of 60 rounds per man. Ahead lay the long retreat towards the Rhine, which was crossed on the night of 9 February, and it was not until the beginning of April that the tattered British regiments reached Bremerhaven, where ships were waiting to transport them back to Britain. According to the regiment's records the retreat was a dreadful experience: 'Food was not to be obtained, the inhabitants were inhospitable; with the enemy in their rear, the snow knee deep, and blown in swirls by the wind into their faces, until they were partially or entirely blinded. Their plight was most pitiable.' Around 350 men of the 78th died or were killed in action.

By the time the 1st battalion returned to Britain – for a time it was stationed at Chelmsford – the 2nd battalion had embarked for service in South Africa, where British forces were in action to seize Dutch possessions including the Cape of Good Hope. Under the command of Lieutenant-Colonel Alexander Mackenzie of Fairburn the battalion took part in the brief fighting at Wynberg, which led to the surrender of Cape Town and the end of the operations. In November the 1st battalion arrived in South Africa and the two battalions were amalgamated prior to a deployment in India. Earlier the 1st battalion had taken part in an unsatisfactory expedition to assist French Royalists on the island of L'Isle Dieu off the coast of Brittany. Although the battalion succeeded in landing, the collapse of the French Royalists meant that the men had to be re-embarked almost immediately and returned to Poole in Dorset.

79TH HIGHLANDERS

The third constituent regiment to be formed was created by Alan Cameron of Erracht, who may justly be described as the 'onlie begetter' of the 79th Highlanders, also styled initially as the Cameronian Volunteers. An experienced soldier who had served the Crown during the American War of Independence – he had been forced to the colonies after killing a neighbour in a duel – Cameron was a shrewd operator who had married well and enjoyed considerable political influence in London. Determined to raise a regiment from Clan Cameron he had to struggle long and hard to get his way and Letters of Service were not issued to him until 17 August 1793. He established his first headquarters at Stirling but commenced recruiting in Cameron territory in Lochaber, Appin, Mull and north Argyll, and by the end of the year had 654 men under his command. The new regiment wore the standard red coatee of the Highland regiments of the time but it was unusual in not wearing government tartan, or a variation of it. Instead it wore a tartan specially designed by Cameron's mother, Marsali Maclean of Drimin, which came to be known as the Cameron Erracht. The original patterns of clothing for the 79th have been lost but Cameron's most recent biographer, Lorraine Maclean of Dochgarroch, argues that the tartan was based on a

Macdonald sett with the omission of two red lines and the addition of a yellow stripe. She also quotes a story from the regimental magazine of 1907 about an argument involving three Black Watch, Seaforth and Cameron privates about the history and traditions of their respective tartans. When the Black Watch private condemns the reddish hue of the Cameron tartan as looking like bully beef he receives the angry retort from the Cameron private that it originated in the Garden of Eden where Adam and Eve clothed themselves in garments of leaves. 'If ye can understand, the leaves faded in coorse o' time, an' took on reddish tints, wi' here an' there a yellow streak. An' there ye can see for yersels whaur the idea o' the Cameron tartan sprang frae.'

Having been passed fit for service following an inspection in Stirling in January 1794, the 79th proceeded to Ireland under Cameron's command and while there the size of the regiment was increased to 1,000. Their next deployment came in the early summer when they were shipped across to Flanders to join the Duke of York's army. As happened to the 1st battalion of the 78th, Cameron's men found themselves caught up in the long retreat back into Germany during one of the most bitterly cold winters on record. In his history of the Highland regiments, Major-General Sir David Stewart of Garth, an eminent Black Watch officer, recorded the hardships facing the men as they pulled back towards the Rhine with the French in pursuit. Not only was it certain death for a man to lie down to sleep, but 'the cold was so intense that brandy froze in bottles, the Highlanders of the 78th, 79th and the new recruits of the 42nd (very young soldiers) wore their kilts and yet the loss was out of comparison less than that sustained by some other corps.' The 79th lost around 200 men, the majority to illness and the extreme weather conditions.

In April the following year the new regiment reached Bremerhaven and returned by troopship to England, where it was stationed at Newport on the Isle of Wight. There was an immediate need to get replacement soldiers for those who had been lost in the recent campaign but instead of getting permission to start recruiting, on 1 July 1795 Cameron received unwelcome news from General William Fawcett, the Adjutant-General. Cameron was to be allowed all his officers and men who were 'real Highlanders to enable you to proceed in raising your regiment afresh' but all others were to be sent as drafts to 40th (later 1st South Lancashire Regiment), 54th (later 2nd Dorset Regiment) and 59th (later 2nd East Lancashire Regiment), which were about to leave for operations in the Caribbean. Cameron insisted that these orders were in breach of his original Letter of Service and the following day he was interviewed by the Duke of York. A tall, heavily built man, Cameron was prepared to stand his ground even though he was in the presence of the army's commander-in-chief and a royal duke.

York's argument was quite simple. The regiments specified needed strengthening, the 79th was a new regiment and he had been told that it had not performed particularly well in Flanders. It was easier and more effective to break it up. At that, Cameron lost his temper and spoke to his superior in a way that regimental commanders should perhaps avoid: 'To draft the 79th is more than you or your royal father dare do.' York was not prepared to budge and replied: 'The king, my father, will certainly send the regiment to the West Indies.' This was tantamount to a death sentence as regiments serving in the Caribbean inevitably suffered huge numbers of casualties from disease and Cameron's response entered the folklore of the 79th. 'You may tell the king, your father, from me, that he may send us to hell if he likes, and I'll go at the head of them, but he daurna' draft us.' By way of compromise York agreed to inspect Cameron's men and after admitting that 'they are a damned good regiment' he declared that he was wrong to hold a bad opinion of them and agreed to rescind the order. It was a close call but it did not save the 79th from York's threat to send them to the West Indies. A week later it sailed from Plymouth, but tragedy overtook Cameron during the voyage when his wife Ann was swept overboard and drowned.

At the time of its arrival in Martinique the 79th consisted of two lieutenant-colonels, one major, six captains, eight lieutenants, eight ensigns, five staff, 35 sergeants, 19 drummers and 479 rank and file. By the end of its deployment two years later 267 of that number had succumbed to disease, a regular and melancholy outcome for British regiments serving in that area of operations at the time. In one week in August, 26 men died of yellow fever but as a visitor to the regiment remembered, Cameron did not allow standards to slip and mess nights remained formal occasions even though the climate might have dictated otherwise. The writer of the following account, John Leach Panter, was a 19 year old whose memoirs were published in *Blackwood's Magazine* in September 1946:

> Upon my introduction to the Colonel [Alan Cameron of Erracht] he gave me a Scotch shake of the hand which very nearly squeezed the blood out of my finger-ends. The party was numerous (about twenty-four) and the dinner and wines excellent, but, during the whole repast, two Scotch bagpipers paced the room, round and round the table, and created such a stunning noise that it was very difficult to hear anybody speak. I, unluckily, showed by my looks some impatience at what I considered a most barbarous intrusion, upon which a hint was given by some means at the table and those bagpipers came, one on each side of me, blowing and playing with all their might, and they literally bothered me entirely. During dinner a great deal of wine was drunk, and upon the removal of the cloth, full sized glasses of brandy, rum, gin and noyeau [fruit-flavoured brandy liqueur] were

handed round for each person to take one, after which the President said, 'Gentlemen, you know my rule, thirteen bumpers, and then every man does as he pleases.'

The author described the huge amounts of alcohol as 'an appalling sentence of death' and was gratified to be excused further imbibing although he noted that Cameron's son, also a 19 year old, drank 'the quantity prescribed and afterwards, to my great surprise, walked arm in arm with me down the hill to the town, quite steadily'. Alas, for Cameron, matters were less steady back in London where the War Office was intent on reducing his regiment by drafting the men into the 42nd Highlanders, which had formed part of a force of some 17,000 soldiers sent to the West Indies under the command of Lieutenant-General Sir Ralph Abercromby to attack French and Dutch holdings in the area, and had suffered a high number of casualties. On this occasion Cameron had no option but to obey orders and he returned home in the summer of 1797 with a cadre of officers and non-commissioned officers to effectively rebuild his regiment from scratch.

CHAPTER TWO

The Global War against France

By the time the eighteenth century came to an end Napoleon
Bonaparte was the undisputed leader of France and most of Europe
was under his control. As a young artillery officer he had come to
prominence in the fighting at Toulon in 1793, and six years later he
was First Consul and virtual leader of France. The war had produced
an interlude with the Treaty of Amiens, which was negotiated in
the winter of 1802–03, but it turned out to be little more than a
truce and it did nothing to dissuade Napoleon from pursuing his
territorial ambitions in Europe. Worse, the conclusion of hostilities
persuaded the British government once again to reduce the size
of its armed forces: plans were put in place to halve the number
of warships and to set the strength of the army at 95,000 soldiers
(plus 18,000 for the Irish garrison). Heightened tensions with
France eventually postponed these unwise economies but the fact
that Britain was prepared to consider defence cutbacks convinced
Napoleon to take a bolder line in his foreign policy. The outbreak
of fresh hostilities was sparked by a disputed claim over possession
of the island of Malta, which had been captured by Britain in 1800
and was a vital strategic base for controlling the Mediterranean.

However, having cowed most of Europe, Napoleon's ultimate aim was to invade Britain with an army 200,000 strong which included the majority of his most experienced field commanders, including the future marshals Bernadotte, Soult and Ney. It was a moment of supreme danger, but in October 1805 the enterprise was foiled by Admiral Lord Nelson's famous victory at Trafalgar, where the French and Spanish fleets were destroyed.

The repercussions were enormous: Napoleon had to give up all hope of invading his most powerful enemy, the Royal Navy had won command of the seas and Britain was given a fresh opportunity to pursue the war against France on the continent of Europe. Before that latter stage could be reached, though, the country had to build up an army capable of taking on and defeating France's seemingly impregnable land forces. To do that, the problem of recruitment had to be addressed, additional funds had to be made available to purchase equipment and the defence budget had to be increased to allow higher rates of pay. As a result the 72nd, 78th and 79th were all permitted to raise second battalions which mainly, though not exclusively, provided drafts for the regiments' 1st battalions. For example, as we shall see, the 2nd battalion of the 78th also saw active service in Sicily and Egypt. Although many of the men were recruited by ballot – a scheme which allowed substitutes to be used in return for financial recompense – the regiments also had to find potential soldiers by the more traditional means of encouraging young men to enlist by accepting the king's shilling. Drink was a common means of luring men into the army, and public houses often doubled up as recruiting offices, with smartly dressed non-commissioned officers offering hospitality and holding out the promise of a life of adventure.

In most respects the complexion of the British Army had changed little since Marlborough's day in the late seventeenth and early eighteenth centuries. Regiments still consisted of ten companies, with eight in the centre and two slightly larger flank companies composed of grenadiers and light infantrymen. Wherever possible, the latter formations were composed of more experienced soldiers with older veterans and newcomers in the centre. The standard weapon was still the smooth-bore flintlock rifle, whose effective range was around 100 yards, which meant that infantry formations had to get close to the opposition before opening fire in disciplined volleys. By far the biggest reform in tactics was the introduction of light infantrymen and the use of more accurate weapons such as the Baker rifle, which allowed its users to be known as 'sharpshooters'. As used by the French, and later by the British, these new elite troops acted as skirmishers and, operating independently ahead of the main forces, they brought greater flexibility to the battlefield by opening gaps and paving the way for the deployment of heavy infantry and cavalry to exploit the expected breakthrough.

72ND HIGHLANDERS

In the initial stages of the war against Napoleonic France the 72nd was deployed on internal security duties in Ireland, where it was stationed variously at Newry, Clonmel, Kilkenny, Fermoy, Dublin and Cork. The regiment's first deployment in Ireland came in the wake of an earlier revolt by the United Irishmen and the continuing threat of invasion by France; as a result the country remained in a state of turmoil. An act of union was passed in January 1801 making Ireland subject to the Westminster parliament, but two years later there was a fresh rising organised and led by Robert Emmett. Catholic emancipation was also an issue. Although Irish Catholics could now vote and enter the professions, they were debarred from standing for parliament and could not hold major offices of state. The failure to deal with these and other issues led to another two centuries of confrontation and civil and political turbulence which would see the descendants of all three constituent regiments of the

Queen's Own Highlanders return regularly to Ireland with the loss of many lives on both sides.

Towards the end of 1805 the 72nd was on the move again, when it formed part of a force despatched to South Africa to secure the Cape from the Dutch. As previously narrated, France's defeat of the Dutch in 1795 forced Britain to send an expedition to South Africa to secure Cape Town and the Cape of Good Hope. One of the conditions of the Treaty of Amiens was that these possessions should be returned to the Dutch but when hostilities broke out again in 1803 the British government feared that it would lose control of the strategic sea route to India (at that time ships bound for India travelled around the Cape of Good Hope). In conditions of great secrecy an army of 7,000 soldiers assembled at Cork under the command of Lieutenant-General Sir David Baird, who had made his name while fighting in the wars against Tipu Sultan in Mysore. Two brigades were formed, one of them designated as the Highland Brigade, which consisted of 71st Highlanders, 72nd Highlanders and 93rd (Sutherland) Highlanders. The second brigade consisted of 24th (later South Wales Borderers), 38th (later 1st South Staffordshire Regiment) and 83rd (later 1st Royal Ulster Rifles), and the infantry was reinforced by a small number of dragoons plus artillery. Command of the naval force was given to Commodore Sir Home Popham, an old friend of Baird's. On 31 August the invasion fleet left for the south Atlantic and following an uneventful voyage arrived in Table Bay on 4 January 1806.

Baird decided on an immediate landing at Lospard's Bay and although there were problems when one of the landing craft overturned, drowning 36 soldiers, the main force was soon ashore and ready to march on Cape Town. During the advance Baird's men came under accurate fire from the Dutch irregular militia but when it became apparent that resistance was futile, the defenders sued for terms on 10 January. Cape Town fell into British hands and detachments of troops were sent to occupy Simonstown, Muisenberg, Wynberg and Stellenbosch. The recapture of the Cape is not one of the great victories in the history of the British Army – the historian Sir John Fortescue makes little of it and chides Baird for giving prominence to the Highland regiments – but it provided a much-needed boost at a time when military successes were few and far between. As a result the 72nd was destined to remain in South Africa as part of the British garrison until 1821 and during that time, in 1809, it lost its Highland status. Between 1810 and 1814 it formed the garrison on the French island of Mauritius and there was a shorter deployment in India in 1815 when the Nepalese or Gurkha War was going badly. This little-known conflict had broken out as a result of a territorial dispute with the Gurkhas, hardy mountaineers who had established themselves in Kathmandu and the valley of Nepal in 1786. From there they had extended their holdings from Sikkim in the east to the River Sutlej in the west, and in so doing they found themselves encroaching on territory held by the East India Company. Trouble flared up in November 1814 and the war began disastrously for the British with the defeat of a force of 3,500 at Kalanga, north of Dehra Dun, where the senior British officer Major-General Sir Robert Gillespie was killed. In the following year fresh forces were assembled under the command of Major-General Sir David Ochterlony with reinforcements from the British Army, but by the time the 72nd arrived in Calcutta the Nepalese were keen to end hostilities. As a result a peace treaty came into being which allowed Nepal to remain an independent kingdom and in time Gurkha regiments were to serve with great honour and distinction in the British Army.

Before leaving South Africa, the 72nd took part in the first of the so-called Kaffir Wars which bedevilled the country for over 100 years. (To modern ears the description sounds racist but the use of the word 'kaffir', for Xhosa, came into being because of

British inability to pronounce the 'click' represented by the letter 'X' in the Bantu language; in time the word was used generally and derogatively, especially by the Dutch, to describe native Africans.) This succession of conflicts with the Xhosa people, cattle-raising tribes of eastern Natal, flared up when Dutch settlers began moving eastwards from the Cape in the 1770s. As the Dutch attempted to create new settlements along the Fish River their incursion led to fighting which lasted from 1817 to 1821. From the 72nd's regimental records it is clear that it was a long and bruising conflict, with the companies stretched out over long distances in dangerous country:

> This proved an arduous and toilsome duty, in a country nearly devoid of resources, infested by savage animals and marauding Kaffirs; the soldiers lived under canvas, were frequently exposed to the inclemency of the weather, especially while constructing new posts, and patrols were constantly moving from station to station; yet the men were preserved, by the care and attention of their officers, remarkably healthy, and the eldest soldiers, who had been long accustomed to the comparative ease and luxury of the service at Mauritius and Cape Town, performed this difficult duty with facility.

The first Kaffir Wars began in 1779 and the fighting did not end until 1878, when Britain annexed the area which had come to be known as Kaffraria. The 72nd left South Africa in December 1821 and arrived back in Britain in March the following year.

78TH HIGHLANDERS

In February 1797 the 78th Highlanders arrived in Calcutta to start a Seaforth connection with India which lasted until 1945, when 1st Seaforth returned from the fighting in Burma to prepare for the invasion of Malaya (called Malaysia since 1963). In time, especially after the Indian Mutiny of 1857–59 when additional British forces were stationed in the country, India became a second home for Britain's regular soldiers. Compared to service in the United Kingdom, life in India for a soldier was 'cushy'. Even the youngest or most recently enlisted private was treated as a 'sahib' and they were generally excused the kind of chores which would have been given to them at home in Britain. Cleaning up barracks was left to the sweepers, Indians did all the work in the cookhouse and the laundry was in the hands of the washer-women. In return a number of words entered the soldiers' vocabulary to be anglicised and used wherever a regiment was posted – buckshee (free, gratis), charpoy (bed), chit (written message), jeldi (hurry up), pukka (proper), tiffin (lunch or midday meal). Apart from taking part in internal security duties or fighting the occasional war on the frontier, the pattern of service for most soldiers was undemanding and mostly pleasant. Route marches along India's long and grimy roads were a regular feature of military life and although these were tedious most soldiers came to terms with the heat and the dust and even came to admire the ever-changing scenery as the regiment marched across the expanse of India.

When the 78th reached India it spent the first six years in Bengal and Oudh. By then Tipu Sultan had been defeated, but the threat from France was no less potent. Within months of the 78th's arrival there was a great scare when Napoleon prepared to invade Egypt for what many British politicians feared might be a prelude to an attack on India through Persia or Afghanistan. Nelson's defeat of the French fleet at Aboukir Bay put paid to that concern but a new threat emerged from the Marathas, who dominated a huge area from the River Sutlej in the north across the Deccan to Hyderabad and Mysore. Although the Maratha rulers formed a loose confederation they controlled large armies, many of which had been trained and equipped by the French and contained French officers. One ruler, Daulat Rao Scindia, had an army 16,000-strong under the command of a French officer, General Pierre Perron, who recruited heavily during the truce brought about by the Treaty of Amiens. Clearly this potential danger had to be addressed, and it was left to the governor-general, the Marquess Wellesley, to devise a plan which would isolate Scindia and Raghuji Bhonsle of Nagpur. Two offensives were planned for 1803 involving 60,000 British and Indian soldiers under the command of Wellesley's brother, Major-General the Hon. Arthur Wellesley (the future Duke of Wellington), and General Sir Gerard Lake, the 60-year-old commander-in-chief in India, who preferred fox-hunting to soldiering. While Lake moved with the main force into the region between the Jumna and the Ganges, Wellesley moved his force from Bombay into Gujarat. The latter force consisted of the 74th and 78th Highlanders, 19th Light Dragoons, three regiments of East India Company cavalry, plus irregular horse and six regiments of Indian infantry.

Wellesley was anxious to start operations and engage Scindia's army before the onset of the monsoon. His first step was to march on his fortress at Ahmednagar, Scindia's only base in the southern Deccan. Following a four-day siege, it fell on 11 July and Wellesley took it over as a rear base for the rest of the operation. Lack of reliable intelligence hampered the next stage and Wellesley had little option but to move cautiously north towards Aurangabad, reckoning that Scindia would take his army towards Hyderabad, plundering as it went. The British and Indian regiments gave chase, often marching up to 50 miles a day. During the pursuit, Wellesley placed a high premium on personal leadership and set a good example which he expected other officers to follow. Colin Campbell, an officer in the 78th, was suitably impressed, writing later: 'I never saw a man so cool and collected as he was the whole time, no man could have shown a better example to the troops than he did.'

At this stage in the campaign Wellesley's intention was simply to find Scindia's army and destroy it, preferably while it was on the move, but unknown to him the Marathas had learned of his approach and were prepared to meet the threat. On the morning of 23 September Wellesley discovered that a large enemy force was lying ahead of him and decided to view the situation for himself. It was not promising: a large force of Marathas had occupied sloping ground in a triangular area between a river and its tributary. Off-putting though the ground was, Wellesley decided to use the element of surprise. The result was one of the decisive battles in the campaign and earned the regiment the right to call itself an 'Assaye Regiment', the others being the two other British regiments which took part. The battle was fought on a steep and rocky tongue of land between the rivers Kaitna and Juah, and Wellesley's small force of 5,000 men was vastly outnumbered by the Maratha army, which included 45,000 men under French command and an artillery force of over 100 guns. Wellesley formed up his men in two lines, the 78th in the first line on the left, with Indian picquets alongside them; the 74th was in the second, on the right, with two Madras battalions, and the cavalry was in the rear. The plan was to swing round in a hammer blow on the enemy's lines and to push them back towards the River Juah, but things did not work out that way. During the advance the Indian picquets advanced too close to the village of Assaye on their right and came under what Wellesley described as a 'a most terrible cannonade'. In his after-battle report Wellesley was brutally honest about what happened next:

> Another bad consequence resulting from this mistake was the necessity of introducing the cavalry into the action at too early a period. I had ordered it to watch the motions of the enemy's cavalry hanging upon our right, and luckily it charged in time to save the remnants of the 74th and the piquets.

In fact, the charge of the 19th Light Dragoons and 4th Native Cavalry saved the day by allowing the infantry to regroup and continue their advance and destroy the enemy's left flank. On Wellesley's left the 78th and the Madras picquets were able to continue their attack and succeeded in silencing the Maratha artillery but, as James Grant Duff points out in his history of the war, the final victory was due to the courage of the Highlanders and their Indian allies as they stood firm under the murderous enfilading fire from Assaye:

> As the British line advanced they passed many individuals of the enemy who either appeared to have submitted, or lay apparently dead. These persons, rising up, turned their guns on the rear of the British line, and after the more important points were secured, it was some time before the firing thus occasioned could be silenced. The enemy's horse hovered round for some time, but when the last body of infantry was broken, the battle was completely decided, and ninety-eight pieces of cannon remained in the hands of the victors. The loss was severe; upwards of one-third of the British troops lay dead or wounded, but they had, considering the circumstances, achieved a triumph more splendid than any recorded in Deccan history.

Later, as a result of 'that glorious occasion', the 74th and 78th were presented with third colours by the East India Company and became the only regiments in the British Army to enjoy that distinction. The original colour presented to the 78th eventually disintegrated but it was replaced in 1889 and can be seen in the regimental museum at Fort George. Despite the heavy defeat it was not the end of the war and the 78th was involved in two further battles against the Marathas, both of which consisted of close-quarter fighting. The Battle of Argaum was fought three months later against Bhonsle's army, and the Marathas were finally defeated when Bhonsle's fortress at Gwalighur fell on 15 December. Two powerful Indian princes had been defeated and the threat posed by the Marathas was at an end. The East India Company now controlled the bulk of central India and the two British infantry regiments had helped to reinforce the reputation of the Highland soldiers as sturdy and courageous troops capable of fighting and surviving in India's demanding climate. The 1/78th remained in India until 1811, mainly on garrison duties in Bombay and the Portuguese colony of Goa.

The next deployment was further east, when it formed part of an expeditionary force despatched to Java, which had fallen under the control of the French following the defeat of the Dutch 16 years earlier. An expedition had been planned in 1801 but was aborted due to the threat posed by Napoleon in Egypt. But now that the danger was over, and following the capture of Mauritius, the British turned their attention once again to expelling the French from Java. Not only did their presence in the area threaten British commercial interests, but the East India Company was keen to establish a presence in what it described as 'the Bengal of the East Indies'. The driving force behind the plan was a thrusting young official in East India House, Thomas Stamford Raffles, who dreamed of creating 'the most splendid prospect which any administration has beheld since our first acquisition of India itself'. Possession of Java would provide lucrative trading possibilities and it would also create a gateway to the China Sea, and Raffles was able to persuade Lord Minto, the new governor-general of India, that the Company should act quickly and decisively against the French in Java. 'From this moment,' he noted in a memorandum quoted in John Keay's history of the East India Company, 'all my views, all my plans, and all my mind were devoted to create an interest towards Java as should lead to its annexation to our Eastern Empire.'

The planning for the operation was overseen by Raffles, who

was also appointed lieutenant-governor of Java once the colony had been secured. The expeditionary force reached Java in July only to find that the French had abandoned the capital, Batavia, and had withdrawn to Weltervreeden, a cantonment three miles from the city. The first fighting took place on 10 August when the British forced the French to withdraw to a new defensive position, Fort Cornelis, which fell a fortnight later and, as this letter in the records from 'a commuted pensioner' makes clear, during the battle the men of the 78th were much impressed by the Malayan soldiers who fought against them:

> Time was precious; the bugle, therefore, once more sounded the charge. We drove their arms aside, and the next moment our swords and bayonets were deeply dyed in blood. Again and again we charged, until the ill-fated Malay regiment was literally cut to pieces. We now halted a short time to recover our energies, and during the time I took a survey of the horrid work we had been about.

During the fighting the British and Indian forces lost 154 killed in action, amongst them Lieutenant-Colonel William Campbell, the commanding officer of the 78th, but these paled into insignificance when the French and native figures were tallied. During the fighting over 6,000 fell into British hands and 1,000 were killed in action. The easy victory seemed to justify Raffles's ambitious plans and the new lieutenant-governor instituted an equally impressive programme of reforms to bring Java into line with the commercial policies of the East India Company. Much of this was done without consultation and was achieved only at huge and, as it would transpire, unnecessary expense as neither the Company nor the British government had any intention of retaining Java other than as a bargaining counter when Napoleon was eventually defeated. As a result the 1/78th remained in the country until 1816, when Java and Malacca were handed back to the Dutch during the peace negotiations following Waterloo.

During the stay on Java the regiment took part in internal security duties, its one offensive action being an operation to unseat the Sultan of Djocjocarta, 'the most violent and intriguing of the native princes', in 1812 when he raised a rebellion against the British presence. As happened so often to regiments stationed in the tropics, the biggest threat came from the climate and diseases and during the five years of the 1/78th's deployment over 600 of the original complement of 1,027 men had become casualties. There was to be more loss of life during the voyage back to India in September 1816. One of the troopships, the *Frances Charlotte*, carrying six companies struck a reef and sank while negotiating the Andaman Islands in the Indian Ocean. Most of the men and their families managed to struggle ashore on the uninhabited island of Preparis but once ashore some of the survivors succumbed to starvation or heatstroke while they waited for rescue. It took five weeks for help to reach them but in addition to the loss of life the regiment also lost its baggage, its records and all of its funds. Once in Calcutta the 1/78th re-mustered and returned to Britain in March 1817. The next stage was Aberdeen, where the 1st and 2nd battalions amalgamated, both battalions having enjoyed very different experiences during the wars against Napoleonic France.

Having been raised in 1804 by Major-General Alexander Mackenzie-Fraser at Fort George, the 2/78th battalion moved south to Hythe in Kent for further training before being deployed to Gibraltar as part of the garrison. In May 1806 the battalion left Gibraltar to join the British forces in Messina for the defence of Sicily. This deployment was brought about by the flight of the king of Naples into British protection following his usurpation by Joseph Bonaparte, Napoleon's brother; if the island fell into French hands it would imperil Britain's hold on the Mediterranean, so the garrison in Messina was increased to 8,000. At the time, the British had hopes of attacking Italy in conjunction with Austria and Russia, using Sicily as a springboard, but their defeat at the hands of Napoleon put paid to that venture and by the time the 2/78th battalion arrived at the end of July the position was in stalemate. This was broken when a British force under the command of General Sir John Stuart crossed over to the Italian mainland to forestall a threatened French invasion. The major battle was fought at Maida in Calabria where Stuart's smaller force defeated the large French army commanded by General Reynier. It is not one of the best-remembered battles in Britain's military history but Stuart's victory was achieved against battle-hardened French troops and helped to prove that Napoleon's army was not invincible. As Major-General Sir David Stewart of Garth explained in his history of the Highland regiments, it was achieved through the disciplined and accurate firepower of the British infantry battalions which took part in the battle:

> The precision with which these two volleys were fired and their effect were quite remarkable. When the clearing of the smoke – there was hardly a breath of wind to dispel it – enabled us to see the French line, the breaks and vacancies caused by the men who had fallen by the fire appeared like a paling of which part had been thrown down or broken. On our side it was so different, that glancing along the rear of the regiment, I counted only fourteen who had fallen to the enemy's fire.

Following the success at Maida the 2/78th returned to Sicily, where it was quartered in the town of Taormina in preparation for a move to Egypt in February 1807 following the decision of the Ottoman Empire to declare war on Russia and Britain. This force of 5,000 duly set sail for Alexandria on 7 March 1807 under the command of Major-General Alexander Mackenzie-Fraser, but unfortunately for all concerned the expedition was a fiasco. Not only did the opposition turn out to be stronger than anticipated, but on 21 April 1807 the 2/78th found itself in a desperate position at El Hamet during the operations to take the town of Rosetta. Three companies of the battalion found themselves surrounded and outnumbered by a larger Turkish force, which included cavalry, and duly paid the price. During the battle the Highlanders fought stubbornly and managed to create a defensive square but as one of the survivors, Sergeant Waters, made clear in his private papers, resistance was well-nigh impossible:

> On our arrival in the square I considered myself perfectly safe; but the danger still pursued us, for no sooner had they satiated their blood-thirsty appetites by viewing their prey and beheading the unfortunate sufferers, who by this time covered the plain, than they instantly bent their course towards the place of our refuge. The square was formed completely, and determinedly resolved to hold out to the last, but was unfortunately formed upon a hill, surrounded by bushes etc, which the enemy soon succeeded in driving our sharpshooters from, which suffered much in retiring to the square. The enemy's foot now having possession of these bushes, from which we could not drive them without diminishing our square, which their cavalry were anxiously waiting for, we began once more to consider our situation perilous. However, I had the gratification to observe that the officers were unanimous in their resolutions to resist to the last extremity.

The losses in the battalion were 159 killed, including the commanding officer Lieutenant-Colonel Patrick MacLeod of Geanies, and the remainder were forced to surrender. Following this misadventure the British force retreated to Alexandria where it remained until September. During that time Mackenzie-Fraser entered into discussions with the Turkish commanders and a truce was agreed which allowed the British to leave Egypt and return to Sicily. The 2/78th battalion sailed for Britain at the end of the year and arrived in Portsmouth in January 1808. From there it made its way back to Scotland, first at Fort George and then in Aberdeen, where it began making preparations to send drafts to the 1st battalion in India. Most of its efforts were put into recruiting and on that score at least, the regimental records claim that it was a successful effort: 'The recruits were of a good description, being all healthy country lads, with dispositions unadulterated, and ready to receive every good impression. They were also what all national corps ought to be, natives of the country whose names they bore.' The battalion remained in Scotland until 1814, and in 1809 took part in the disastrous operations against the French at Walcheren in Flanders. Not only did the British expeditionary force fail in its objective to destroy the French fleet which lay at anchor in Flushing, but hundreds of soldiers fell victim to fever. By September 4,000 had died (10 per cent of the total) and the force was evacuated.

79TH HIGHLANDERS

On the 79th's return from the Caribbean the regiment was soon back to full strength and took part in the Duke of York's joint British–Russian campaign in the Netherlands, serving in a brigade commanded by Brigadier-General (later Lieutenant-General Sir) John Moore, a Glasgow-born soldier who was one of the coming men in the British Army. Aged 37 at the time, he was very much a soldier's soldier, who believed in the value of training and always put the needs of his men first. In common with other great leaders he argued that all ranks should share the privations and dangers of service in the field, and he was insistent that soldiers in authority should not order their men to do anything unless they were also prepared to carry out the same duty. Above all, he was committed to the regimental system, seeing unit cohesion as the best means of maintaining morale and instilling discipline. 'It is evident that not only the soldiers but that each individual soldier knows what he has to do,' he remarked after inspecting his old regiment, the 52nd Foot. 'Discipline is carried on without severity, the officers are attached to the men and the men to the officers.'

The initial stages of the campaign achieved early success, with the speedy deployment of the allied army at Den Helder and the equally rapid capture of the Dutch fleet off Texel Island but thereafter matters did not run so smoothly. There was a lack of cooperation between the British and Russian field commanders, the Dutch were indifferent at best and hostile at worst to the arrival of their supposed liberators and there was a worrying shortage of artillery pieces. The one major battle involved a frontal attack on the French positions at Egmont-op-Zee on 2 October when the 79th went into the attack with the 25th Foot (later King's Own Scottish Borderers). Their efforts and those of the supporting British regiments were hindered by the use of *tirailleurs*, skirmishing sharpshooters whose accuracy of fire and speed of movement caused high casualties amongst the advancing British redcoats. Similar troops, known as *Jäger,* had served in the Austrian and Prussian armies earlier in the century and had fought under British command in America, and the usefulness of these light troops encouraged the British Army to found a Corps of Riflemen in 1800. A number of officers and men from the 2nd battalion were transferred to the new regiment, which later fought as The Rifle Brigade (95th Regiment), made distinctive by innovations such as rifle-green uniforms with black buttons, bugle commands and a rapid marching pace.

Before the fighting at Egmont-op-Zee commenced there was some confusion in the ranks of the 79th when one of the Highland officers was heard to say, 'The French are our old friends, and of our own race.' Hearing this reference to the Auld Alliance, the age-old friendship between the Scots and the French, Cameron brought his men forward and gave the simple order: 'Now, my men, there they are, and if you don't kill them, by God they will kill you.' The order was understood and the 79th's casualties were comparatively light: two officers and 13 soldiers killed in action. A week later, much to the disgust of the British soldiers, who believed that they had won the upper hand, the Cabinet ordered the withdrawal of York's force and the 79th spent the rest of the year at Chelmsford.

Their next engagement took place in 1801, which turned out to be a year of triumph for the allies. At home William Pitt the Younger resigned as prime minister following his attempt to bring in Catholic emancipation, but the war saw Nelson's victory over the French fleet at Copenhagen and General Sir Ralph Abercromby's successful expedition to engage Napoleon's army of the east in Egypt in 1801. This was designed to oust French forces from Egypt and to relieve the threat which they posed to Britain's holdings in India, but the operation was hazardous. Not only were the French already in position at Alexandria but they had more artillery and possessed cavalry. They were also in a position to oppose the amphibious landings, but thanks to strict training in advance of the landings the British force came safely ashore at Aboukir Bay and was able to repel the main French attack on 21 March. Under Moore's operational direction – he was by then a major-general – the defending British forces showed great coolness under fire and a month later Alexandria was in their hands. To recognise their courage all the regiments involved in the expedition, including the

79th, were granted the right to bear on their colours the figure of the Sphinx superscripted with the word 'Egypt'. As a result of the Battle of Aboukir Bay, Egypt was saved.

Having served with distinction under Abercromby and Moore the 79th was deployed on Minorca, which remained its base until the following year when it returned to home quarters, first in Scotland and second in Ireland. The regiment was in action again in the autumn of 1807, when it formed part of a British force despatched to Denmark to occupy Zealand and to prevent the Danish fleet falling into French hands. At the time Napoleon was intent on enforcing the Continental System, a total blockade of Britain, and the possession of the Danish ships would have aided his efforts. During the operation under the command of Lord Cathcart, the 79th was brigaded with the 92nd Highlanders (later 2nd Gordon Highlanders) and also took part in an expedition to Sweden the following year, when King Gustavus requested allied military support. (In the event this was not required. Gustavus was of unsound mind, tried to arrest Moore and launched an invasion of Norway.)

A number of non-operational incidents stand out from that period. In 1804 the designation of the 79th was changed to 79th Cameronian Highlanders and two years later, to avoid confusion with the 26th (Cameronian) Regiment, this was changed, again, to 79th Cameron Highlanders. In the year of the first name change the War Office suggested to Cameron of Erracht that his regiment should cease wearing the kilt but the idea was given short shrift by the regiment's founder. On 27 October 1804 he wrote to the War Office making it perfectly clear that he had no intention of following the advice:

> I feel no hesitation in saying that the proposed alteration
> must have proceeded from a whimsical idea, more than
> from the real comfort of the Highland soldier, and a wish

to lay aside that national garb, the very sight of which has, upon many occasions, struck the enemy with terror and confusion – and now metamorphose the Highlander from his real characteristic appearance and comfort in an odious incompatible dress, to which it will, in my opinion, be difficult to reconcile him, as a poignant grievance to, and a galling reflection upon Highland corps &c, as levelling that martial distinction by which they have been hitherto *noticed and respected.*

In common with other Highland regiments, a 2nd battalion was raised in 1804, its first commanding officer being Alan Cameron's eldest son, Lieutenant-Colonel Phillips Cameron. It remained in being until August 1815, when its commanding officer was Cameron's second son, Lieutenant-Colonel Nathaniel Cameron.

CHAPTER THREE

The Peninsula, Waterloo and the Long Peace

To complete Napoleon's plans for the Continental System it was essential that France should shut off the Iberian peninsula. After the renewal of hostilities in 1803 France quickly defeated Prussia, Austria and Russia and to complete the domination of Europe Napoleon turned his attention to Spain and Portugal. The first was subjugated by forcing the Spanish king, Charles IV, to abdicate and imposing military rule on the country under Napoleon's brother Joseph. Portugal, England's oldest ally, was then invaded from Spain by an army commanded by Marshal Junot. Both were daring, if ruthless, plans but both were foiled by the refusal of the people of Spain and Portugal to accept French domination and by the British decision to send forces under the command of Arthur Wellesley to assist them in resisting the invasion. The first part of the campaign ended in farce. Following a stunning victory at Vimiero on 21 August 1808 the French army was allowed to retreat back to France in ships provided by the Royal Navy. The agreement sickened Wellesley, who remarked that his officers were free to 'go and shoot red-legged partridges', and it allowed Napoleon to assume command of military operations in the Peninsula. At the same time a new army, under Moore's command, marched from Lisbon into northern Spain through Salamanca towards Valladolid, his aim being to link up with friendly Spanish forces. Backing for the enterprise was provided by 17,000 additional troops under the command of David Baird, whose forces landed in Corunna in October. With the 72nd stationed in South Africa and the 1/78th in the Far East, only the 79th took part in the long campaign to defeat Napoleon's forces in Europe, although in the latter stages the 2/78th saw active service in Holland and Belgium in 1814 and 1815.

On 25 August 1808 the 79th arrived in Lisbon, where Alan Cameron was given a brigade and command passed to his son Phillips, who took the regiment into Spain. Almost immediately things started to go awry. Not only were the British forces ill-prepared to make a long incursion into Spain, but the French had not been idle. Napoleon had assembled a huge army of 250,000 men and in December he moved rapidly against Moore's smaller force of 20,000, taking with him 80,000 crack troops of the 'Old Guard' and two of his most skilled marshals, Soult and Ney. The French moved fast and boldly towards the north-west and by the time that Moore reached Salamanca he realised that not only was he badly outnumbered – Baird had been delayed and did not disembark until the beginning of November – but that Napoleon was now within striking distance. Initially Moore had hoped to attack a smaller French force under Soult at Burgos, but the move only stung Napoleon into a greater determination to crush the British. On Christmas Eve Moore received further intelligence of Napoleon's intentions: the French army had crossed the Guadarrama mountains and was less then 20 miles away. If Moore continued he would risk annihilation and so the order was given to fall back on Corunna, where the navy had been ordered to evacuate them.

So began an epic retreat across the snow-covered mountains. It was an operation which demonstrated great courage and determination but it was also marred by scenes of drunken rampaging as the British soldiers looted the areas through which they passed. In a general order issued on 27 December Moore told his men that he could 'feel no mercy towards officers who neglect, in times like these, essential duties, or towards soldiers who injure the country they are sent to protect', but the regimental records show that in this respect there was no need for the strictures to extend to the 79th, who

> maintained their discipline and efficiency to the end ... the men bore the severe fatigue and privations of the march with fortitude and resolution, and were ever ready to repulse the attacks of the French troops, who from first to last harassed our exhausted columns.

By the year's end Moore's army had passed through the relative safety of Astorga and when Napoleon arrived in the same place on New Year's Day he realised that there would be no pitched battle, as his enemy had made good its escape. Instead of continuing the pursuit he left the rest of the operation in the hands of Ney and Soult and, having been warned of a plot against him, returned to Paris. Two weeks later Moore reached Corunna to find that the fleet had been delayed. There was now no option but to engage the French; during the hard-fought battle Moore was mortally wounded and was carried to a rear area by Guardsmen and men of the 42nd. Like Nelson, he died hoping that he had done his duty – as indeed he had. Of the 30,000 British soldiers who marched into Corunna and engaged the French in battle some 24,000 were eventually evacuated.

Following its return to Britain the regiment was part of the force which took part in the expedition to capture the island of

Walcheren in Flanders in July 1809. As we have seen, not only did it fail to achieve its military objective but over 4,000 soldiers fell victim to fever. Astonishingly, or perhaps because of good medical practice, the 79th was relatively unscathed, leaving the regimental surgeon Dr Anderson to record:

> In 1809 the 79th accomplished what no other regiment did. In January of that year they were in Spain at the Battle of Corunna, and returned to England in February, when 700 men and several officers suffered from a dangerous typhus fever, yet not a man died. In July they embarked 1,002 bayonets for Walcheren, were engaged during the whole siege of Flushing in the trenches, yet had not a man wounded, and whilst there, lost only one individual in fever – Paymaster Baldock, the least expected of anyone. During the three months after their return to England only ten men died, and in December of that same year again embarked for the Peninsula, 1,032 strong.

For the next three years the British Army and its allies were involved in a war of movement and attrition as Wellesley engaged the enemy whenever it was prudent and showed that he knew 'when to retreat and to dare to do so'. Throughout the campaign Wellesley was uncomfortably aware that defeat would not only lead to disaster for Britain, but would allow Napoleon to remove his troops for service elsewhere in Europe. 'As this is the last army England has,' noted Wellesley, 'we must take care of it.' The 79th arrived in Lisbon in January 1810 and was immediately sent to form part of the garrison at Cadiz, which was under siege by French forces led by Marshal Claude Victor, the conqueror of General Don Gregorio Garcia de la Cuesta's Spanish army at Medellin. During the summer the strategic situation was changed by France's earlier defeat of Austria, which allowed the French to redouble their efforts in the Peninsula. With the Spanish forces rapidly disintegrating, Wellesley (now ennobled as Viscount Wellington) decided that it would be prudent to concentrate his efforts on the defence of Portugal. As part of that readjustment the 79th returned to Lisbon, where it was brigaded with 7th Foot (later Royal Fusiliers) and 61st Foot (later 2nd Gloucestershire Regiment) under the command of Alan Cameron, now a major-general.

It was not long before the 79th was in action. To block the advance of a large French army under the command of Marshal Massena, Wellington had moved his forces along the Sierra de Busaco, where Cameron's brigade formed the right of the line. At dawn on 27 September French *tirailleurs* engaged the British picquets, which were commanded by Captain Alexander Cameron of the 79th and during the fighting, much of it close-quarter, Cameron was killed along with seven of his men and another officer, and 41 men were wounded. Wellington hoped that by checking Massena at Busaco he would hold up the French advance, but the enemy's weight of numbers encouraged him to retire behind the formidable defensive positions known as the Lines of Torres Vedras. The move forced Massena to retreat to Santaram and both armies went into winter quarters. Operations did not begin again until March when Wellington invested the frontier fortress of Almeida, a ploy which tempted Massena to move against him; the result was the Battle of Fuentes d'Onor, which was fought between 3 and 5 May 1811.

When the French forces arrived they found Wellington's army of British, Portuguese and Spanish regiments deployed on a line which stretched from the village of Fuentes d'Onor in Spain, to Villa Formosa on the Portuguese side of the border, on a rocky plateau between the small rivers Dos Casas and Turones. The first French moves were made against the British positions at Fuentes d' Onor, where the defences had been entrusted to the 71st and 79th

Highlanders and the 24th Foot (later The South Wales Borderers), all under the command of Lieutenant-Colonel Phillips Cameron. During a fiercely contested French onslaught the British battalions were forced to retire before regrouping near the village chapel, where they were reinforced by the 88th Foot (later 1st Connaught Rangers). As a result they were able to drive back the French but during this phase of the fighting Colonel Cameron was killed by a French rifleman. His death prompted a cry of grief from the men of the 79th – 'Thuit an Comsbronach' ('Cameron Has Fallen') – and according to Percy Groves's history they reacted quickly and decisively: 'Maddened with rage, the Highlanders rushed upon the French; the man who had shot their beloved colonel was bayoneted – his officer met with a like fate; and a desperate hand-to-hand fight ensued in which the Highlanders and their comrades well maintained their ground.' Cameron was not just a popular officer, he was also the son of the founder of the regiment and his death was widely mourned, not least by the writer Sir Walter Scott, who commemorated the incident in his poem 'The Vision of Don Roderick':

> And what avails thee that, for Cameron slain,
> Wild from his plaided ranks the yell was given?
> Vengeance and grief gave mountain-range the rein,
> And, at the bloody spear-point headlong driven,
> The despot's giant guards fled like the rack of heaven.

Together with another victory at Albuera a few weeks later the 1811 campaign was a turning point for the British and their Portuguese allies, and paved the way for the liberation of Spain. Ahead lay the battles of Ciudad Rodrigo, Badajoz, Vitoria and Salamanca, which led to the French gradually pulling out of Spain. All were hard-pounding battles but, having been placed in the reserve on account of illness in the ranks and the 287 casualties suffered at Fuentes d'Onor, the 79th took part only in the latter battle, which was fought on 22 July 1812. The victory allowed Wellington to capture Madrid and to begin the siege of Burgos, which housed the bulk of the French strategic reserves. Before beginning the siege proper on 19 September the enemy's outworks had to be cleared and the task was entrusted to a 'forlorn hope' composed of light companies under the command of Major the Hon. E.C. Cocks of the 79th. Although they succeeded in gaining possession of the horn-work on St Michael's Mount, the French retired into Burgos's solid fortifications, Wellington's forces were unable to make any further progress and the siege was abandoned on 21 October. During the operations the 79th lost three officers (including Cocks) and 28 soldiers killed and five officers and 85 soldiers wounded.

The regiment then went into winter quarters with the rest of Wellington's army and on the resumption of hostilities it was transferred to Major-General Sir Edward Pakenham's 6th Division. On joining them the 79th took part in the Battle of the Pyrenees on 28 July 1813, when a superior French force was defeated at bayonet-point. ('With great slaughter' according to Groves.) The victory forced the French to retreat over the border back to France with the British in hot pursuit and the year ended with further French defeats at Nivelle (9 November) and the valley of the Nive (10 December). Now brigaded with the 42nd and 91st (Argyll) Highlanders, the 79th fought in the last battle of the campaign at Toulouse, where a French force under Marshal Soult was decisively defeated on 10 April 1814. This was followed by the news that Paris had fallen to the allies and Louis XVIII had been restored to the throne of France. With hostilities in Europe at an end the 79th left for Cork, which it reached on 26 July, and started preparations for joining the garrison in North America. Contrary winds twice prevented the convoy from setting sail, and under the circumstances this proved to be a good thing.

On 26 February 1815, while the 79th was in Belfast, Napoleon broke out of his exiled imprisonment in Elba and set about reclaiming his position. Using the magic of his name he rallied the veterans of his old armies and challenged the rest of Europe to respond to his latest bid for power. The result was the Waterloo campaign, which led to his defeat at the hands of the British and the Prussians but, as Wellington remarked after his final triumph over the French emperor, it had been a close-run thing. Britain and its allies had lost 16,000 casualties, the Prussians lost 7,000 and the French losses were computed at 25,000. Fought on 18 June 1815, the Battle of Waterloo put an end to Napoleon's ambitions – afterwards he was exiled on the Atlantic island of St Helena – and it is counted as one of the greatest battles ever fought by the British Army. The triumph is made more memorable by the fact that Wellington was outnumbered, his British troops had been depleted – 14,000 Peninsula veterans had been sent to America – and many of the allied German and Dutch soldiers were inexperienced. Against his enemies' advantages, Wellington enjoyed close cooperation with the Prussian commander, Field Marshal Blücher, and as a result of this cohesion allied intelligence about the French dispositions was more accurate.

During the operations the 79th served in Major-General Sir Thomas Picton's 5th Division and fought with it in the opening phase of the battle at Quatre Bras, a small hamlet on the intersection of the roads to Brussels, Charleroi, Nivelles and Namur. The arrival of the 79th was later commemorated by Lord Byron in Canto III of his poem *Childe Harold's Pilgrimage*:

> And wild and high the 'Cameron's Gathering' rose,
> The war-note of Lochiel, which Albyn's hills
> Have heard, and heard too, have her Saxon foes –
> How in the noon of night that pibroch thrills

Savage and shrill! But with the breath which fills
Their mountain-pipe, so fill the mountaineers
With the fierce native daring which instils
The stirring memory of a thousand years,
And Evan's [Ewan Cameron], Donald's [Donald Cameron
of Lochiel] fame rings in each clansman's ears!

At Quatre Bras the regiment was on the extreme left of the British line south of the Namur road and went into the attack at four o'clock in the afternoon of 16 June, demonstrating speed and aggression which discomfited the opposition and forced it to retire. By nightfall the battle was still evenly balanced but the following day Picton was able to deploy his division onto a superior position on the ridge near the farm of La Haye Sainte, where the 79th held the centre with the 28th Foot (later 1st Gloucestershire Regiment). In the initial stages of the fighting Picton was killed and his division came under sustained attack by the French cavalry, forcing the infantry to strengthen its defensive squares. To stiffen morale at this desperate moment Piper Kenneth Mackay struck up the traditional rallying tune 'Cogadh no Sith' ('War or Peace, the Gathering of the Clans'). It was an action of supreme heroism, as he stood outside the square while he was playing his pipes and presented an easy target to the enemy. During the Battle of Waterloo, fought on 18 June, the 79th lost four officers and 29 soldiers killed and nine officers and 132 soldiers wounded, but it was also singled out for special praise by Wellington in his despatch on the conduct of the battle. The only other regiments to be distinguished in this way were the 28th Foot and the 42nd and 92nd Highlanders. Following the victory the 79th formed part of the army of occupation in Paris and did not return to Britain until November the following year when it was posted on home service at Chichester.

72ND HIGHLANDERS

On the regiment's return to Britain from South Africa it received the happy news that it had once again become a Highland regiment. The order was given by King George IV on 19 December 1823 but it contained the stipulation 'that the Officers and Men shall wear trews instead of kilts', the chosen tartan being the Royal Stuart in the Prince Charles Edward Stuart's sett, which was worn until 1881. At the same time the regiment was given a new title, 72nd or Duke of Albany's Own Highlanders, the designation coming in honour of HRH Prince Frederick Augustus, Duke of York and Albany, second son of King George II and the commander-in-chief of the British Army. For the next five years the 72nd remained on home service in Scotland, Ireland and England before returning to South Africa in 1828. Once again it was involved in offensive operations against the Xhosa, receiving the battle honour 'South Africa 1835' for its part in what was described as 'continuous guerrilla warfare against the predatory tribesmen' who had been carrying off the white settlers' cattle.

In 1840 the regiment returned to Britain, where it spent four years on internal security duties in England and Ireland. During the course of its deployment in England the 72nd was involved in the disagreeable task of giving aid to the civil powers during a period of unrest in Lancashire's industrial towns in 1842. Much of the agitation was caused by the economic depression which was sweeping the country as unemployment rose to 60 per cent and the poor were evicted from their homes. Wages were cut and there was an eruption of strike action which was also fomented by political agitation created by the Chartists, early socialists who demanded universal male suffrage, the removal of the property qualification for membership of parliament and the redrawing of electoral districts. Although the movement lacked a central organisation and was largely ineffective the government took fright at the huge demonstrations it inspired throughout 1842 and responded with a heavy hand. On a number of occasions the 72nd was ordered to fire into crowds at Preston and Blackburn. Some idea of the predicament facing the 72nd can be found in a description of a workers' demonstration written by a reporter in the *Morning Chronicle*:

> The sight was just one of those which it is impossible to forget. They came pouring down the wide road in their thousands, taking up its whole breadth – a gaunt, famished-looking desperate multitude, armed with huge bludgeons, flails, pitchforks and pikes, many without coats and hats . . . as they marched they thundered out to a grand old tune a stirring melody:
>
> > 'Men of England, ye are slaves,
> > Though ye rule the roaring waves,
> > Though ye shout from sea to sea,
> > "Britons everywhere are free".'

The last year of the home posting was spent in Ireland and between 1844 and 1848 the regiment was based in Gibraltar together with the 79th Highlanders. Following four years' service the regiment deployed to the Caribbean where the main bases were Trinidad and Barbados, with detachments based in St Lucia, Demerara, Grenada and Tobago. As happened so often to British regiments based in the West Indies the main problems were illness and disease and the 72nd proved no exception. In the first year alone the regiment lost four officers and 59 soldiers to yellow fever. Some idea of the problems facing regiments in the West Indies can be found in the fact that it took 11 years to repair the condemned barracks at Orange Grove in Trinidad and 20 years to build new barracks at Fort Charlotte in the Bahamas. In an attempt to address this problem – for years the

Caribbean had been a death-trap for the regiments of the British Army – the War Office introduced a regular rotation of regiments. Shorter tours of duty were ordered for the most insalubrious spots and a new pattern of service was introduced whereby regiments were sent to the Mediterranean for acclimatisation before being posted to the heat and humidity of the West Indies or North America. Later this would be extended to the eastern hemisphere, where regiments spent time in Australia or South Africa before proceeding to India or Ceylon (now Sri Lanka). Between 1839 and 1853 the British Army suffered 58,139 casualties to disease or illness, and contemporary War Office papers reveal that the annual death rates per 1,000 men were 33 for non-commissioned officers and men and 16.7 for officers (in Jamaica it was 69 per 1,000 for officers and men).

At the same time steps were taken to reduce the burden on the British Army by raising colonial corps and cutting back the number of garrisons in colonies which, it was reasoned, could just as easily be protected by the new generation of steam-powered warships of the Royal Navy. In the summer of 1851 the 72nd moved north to Halifax in Canada, where there had been serious outbreaks of rioting in Montreal. Earlier, in 1842, there had been a dispute with the United States over the Maine–New England border and this had been followed in 1846 by a similar dispute over the Oregon border. All these problems meant that Britain had to maintain a sizable North American garrison of 5,000 troops throughout the period, and there was no substantial reduction in Canada until after the American Civil War of 1861–65, when fears of US territorial aggrandisement started to subside.

While the 72nd was in Canada a crisis in the Balkans and the Levant in 1853 led to a confrontation with Russia on the one hand and Britain, France and the Ottoman Empire on the other. The following year the conflict known as the Crimean War broke out (see Chapter Four), but to the regiment's chagrin it remained in Canada until October 1854, when its depot companies were based in Ireland to recruit men for the 42nd and 79th Highlanders who were already engaged in the fighting. By the end of the year the regiment was 300 men under strength but such was the casualty rate in the Crimea – mainly due to disease, illness and death from wounds – that the 72nd was ordered to sail to what was being described in the British press as 'the seat of war' and was posted to Malta in January 1855.

78TH HIGHLANDERS

At the beginning of the long peace which ended the Napoleonic Wars the 78th was stationed in Ireland, where it received its third stand of colours in 1818. In October that year the Highland Society of London presented the regiment with 25 copies of *Fragments of Ancient Poetry Collected in the Highlands of Scotland and Translated from the Gaelic or Erse Language* (the Poems of Ossian), written by James Macpherson. The chairman of the society asked the commanding officer to dispose the copies 'as he may judge most expedient, and as best calculated to promote the views of the society', adding the hope that the regiment would 'continue to cherish, as it now does, the noble sentiments of the patriotic Ossian'. Colonel MacLeod reciprocated by thanking the society but it could have been a tricky moment because Macpherson's reputation was still a matter of controversy. When the Ossian poems appeared in 1760 they had caused a sensation about their authenticity, with Dr Samuel Johnson and other critics declaring them to be fraudulent. Following an investigation by the Highland Society of London in 1796 it was acknowledged that Macpherson had pieced together fragments from original sources with passages of his own creation but, despite the controversy, Macpherson's Ossian had a profound effect on the way in which the Highlands of Scotland were viewed in the early nineteenth century.

In 1821 the 78th was on parade in Dublin for the state visit of King George IV and had the honour of being one of the three kilted Highland regiments present, the others being the 42nd and the 93rd Highlanders. In 1826 the regiment sailed for Ceylon, which was to be its home for the next 11 years. The island had first attracted British interest during the Seven Years War, when Trincomalee was briefly occupied, but the main period of colonial influence began in 1795 when British troops landed to take over the areas of Dutch control. For a while the island was run by the East India Company and became a Crown Colony in 1798. This was confirmed by the Treaty of Amiens in 1802 and in 1814 a rebellion by Sinhalese chiefs of Kandy against their Tamil king resulted in further British military deployments. The king was deposed and his territories annexed a year later. Although Ceylon was considered to be a pleasant posting there was the ever-present risk of disease and bad health and during its years on the island the 78th lost 299 officers and men, mainly to cholera.

The first three years were spent in Kandy, where the regiment gained a high reputation for its discipline and good conduct, so much so that the civic authorities were moved to comment on their departure in August 1831 that 'no complaint had ever been made of ill-treatment or injustice by them to any of the natives'. While in the next station at Trincomalee cholera struck once again and in one 48-hour period in the autumn of 1832 the 78th lost 25 men before the outbreak subsided at the beginning of November. The regiment remained in Ceylon until 1837, when it sailed back to Britain on board the troopships *Numa* and *Barossa*. So depleted was the regiment by that stage that its full complement consisted of a lieutenant-colonel, five captains, nine subalterns, three regimental staff, 30 sergeants, 10 drummers and 363 soldiers. Also travelling with the 78th was a young elephant which had been presented to them by the 58th Foot (later 2nd Northamptonshire Regiment) and had been trained to march at the head of the pipe band. It was a relevant choice of beast: an elephant superscribed ASSAYE appeared on the regiment's colours and, later, provided the collar badges for the Queen's Own Highlanders. Later the beast was presented to the Zoological Society of Edinburgh.

On its return to Britain the regiment was stationed in Ireland, where it provided drafts for the garrison in Canada and was once more so depleted that it was ordered to return to Scotland to begin recruiting. By the summer of 1840 it was back up to strength and was sent to the north of England to provide aid to the civil authorities to deal with the demonstrations caused by the industrial unrest of the period (see above). The following year the 78th returned to Ireland in November but no sooner had it arrived than it was ordered to prepare for an emergency posting to India. Reinforcements were received from various regiments including the 72nd, 79th, 92nd and 93rd Highlanders and the embarkation on six troopships was exceptionally hurried, due to the disastrous news coming out of the country. In one of the greatest military disasters ever to befall the British Army a brigade-sized force of some 4,500 British and Indian soldiers together with 12,000 camp followers was massacred while withdrawing from Kabul in Afghanistan in January 1842.

The catastrophe was the climax of a policy to gain control of Afghanistan as a buffer to prevent Russian expansionism which might threaten Britain's holdings in India but the plans were badly thought out and the whole operation was dogged by a lack of political will and insufficient funding. In the spring of 1839 a joint British and Indian force had crossed into Sind and marched up the Bolan Pass to take Kandahar, which fell without a battle. A British puppet ruler, Shah Shuja, was then placed on the throne and his rival, Dost Muhammad, was forced to flee. It should have been the beginning of a settled rule but due to lack of money and muddled thinking in London the British garrison withdrew from Kabul at the end of 1841. This encouraged the Afghans to oppose Shah Shuja and the British quickly lost control in Kabul. A combination of atrocious winter weather, poor planning and Afghan duplicity led to the force's complete destruction. Despite Afghan promises of safe conduct through the passes to Peshawar the column was attacked and the only survivor was Dr William Brydon, an army surgeon, who managed to ride into the frontier fort at Jalalabad bearing the dreadful news.

British opinion was outraged by the disaster and reinforcements were rushed out to India to lend assistance to the remaining Afghan garrisons at Jalalabad and Kalat-i-Ghilzai. In fact they would not be needed, as Britain decided to abandon its Afghan policy and it was not until 1878 that there was further imperial involvement in the affairs of this mountainous and remote country (see Chapter Five). Nevertheless, the 78th proceeded as planned to India and was based at Poona until the following year, when it was ordered to march first to Karachi and then to Sukkur in Sind. While in the latter station the 78th was ravaged by one of the worst outbreaks of cholera experienced by a British regiment. In the course of 1844, 535 officers and men succumbed to the disease, as well as 202 wives and children. The regimental records contain a moving description of the way in which the men of the 78th dealt with the outbreak as the survivors made their way back to Bombay:

> The medical men attributed the sickness in a great degree to the improper time at which the regiment was moved, and the malaria engendered by the head of the sun on the swampy plains which had been overflowed by the Indus. The deaths continued very frequent all the time we remained, and at last, on the 21st and 24th of December 1844 we embarked, or rather the men crawled on board

common country boats, which conveyed us to Hyderabad. These boats were very imperfectly chuppered [roofed with straw or reed]. The sun struck through the thatching by day, and the very heavy dews penetrated it at night, when it was extremely cold. When we moored in the evening we used to bury our dead . . . We put layers of thorns inside, around and on top of the graves in hopes of preserving the remains of our poor comrades from the attacks of the troops of jackals swarming in the neighbourhood. There were no stones to be had, so thorns and bushes well beaten down were all the protection we could give.

The regiment quickly recovered from this disaster with drafts from other regiments, including 100 from the 2nd Foot (later The Queen's Royal Regiment) and for the next four years was based in the Bombay Presidency at Poona, Kirkee and Belgaum. As a result of the epidemic and its aftermath there were now more English and Irish soldiers than Scottish soldiers but they quickly settled in and happily adopted the traditions and customs of a Highland regiment. Between 1839 and 1853 the 78th was detached to Aden, a hot and inhospitable garrison in south Arabia which provided little but an exercise in monotony with occasional skirmishes against Arab tribesmen loyal to the Sultan of Lahej. In one engagement Lieutenant Delisser was attacked while riding to Steamer Point; having dismounted he engaged his assailant, seized his sword and decapitated him. The corpse was subsequently hung in chains at the entrance of the fortifications as a warning to others. One happier result of the deployment was the creation of the well-known and aptly named pipe tune 'The Barren Rocks of Aden' by Piper James Mauchline of the 78th. For many years it was the traditional interval tune played at half-time by the pipe band of the Queen Victoria School during international rugby matches at Murrayfield in

Edinburgh. In 1853 the 78th returned to Poona, which was to be its home until 1857, when it formed part of a force commanded by Lieutenant-General Sir James Outram sent to the Persian Gulf to deter the Shah of Persia from forming an alliance with Russia. Having landed at Bushire, Outram's forces engaged and routed the Persians at Koosh-ab and at Mohomrah on the Shatt-al-Arab waterway. The 78th returned to India in May 1857 to find the country once more on the brink of a major catastrophe.

79TH HIGHLANDERS

Following its exertions in the war against France, the 79th spent the next seven years on home service before being sent to Canada in August 1825. This was to be its home for the next three years, with detachments based in Kingston and Toronto. In September 1836 it returned to Britain for a further period of home service which saw the men taking part in frequently disagreeable internal security duties in the north of England during the period of industrial unrest in 1839. Gibraltar was the regiment's next base, a monotonous posting which lasted from 1841 to 1848, when the 79th re-crossed the Atlantic for a fresh deployment at Quebec which lasted until the summer of 1851. All this was very different from the excitements of active service, and with time hanging heavily on the soldiers' hands the regiment's officers organised hobbies and pastimes such as amateur dramatics. To begin with the performances were limited to the schoolroom in the garrison, but such was the enthusiasm displayed by the thespians in the 79th that they moved to the town's theatre where, according to the regimental records, they gave 'one or two performances of the national drama "Rob Roy" in a manner which would not have disgraced the boards of many a provincial theatre at home'. One player was a particular star, a bandsman whom the records, with admirable discretion, refer to only as 'C'. His speciality was an interpretation of the character Bailie Nichol Jarvie, one of Sir Walter Scott's more inspired fictional creations in his novel *Rob Roy*, and the bandsman quickly became a firm favourite of the audience, many of whom were of Scots descent and were keen to treat him in the customary way. As the records reveal, the inevitable happened:

> One fine morning, as the commanding officer [Lieutenant-Colonel the Hon. Lauderdale Maule], accompanied by the adjutant and one or two other officers, was crossing the barrack square on his way to the orderly-room, the party encountered the unfortunate quondam Thespian in a state of considerable elevation, between two men of the guard, who were conveying him to durance vile. As his dim eye fell on the form of the commanding officer, a gleam of tipsy humour for a moment lighted up his somewhat grotesque lineaments. John Barleycorn [whisky] had, for the time, extinguished all terrors of his august presence. 'Hang a bailie!' hiccupped poor C as he passed the group, who were carefully ignoring his vicinity. 'Hang a bailie ma conscience!' It is scarcely necessary to say that when brought up for judgement some four-and-twenty hours afterwards the unfortunate magistrate was dealt with as lightly as the code of military discipline permitted.

In 1851 the 79th returned to Scotland, where it was based first at Stirling and then at Edinburgh. Two years later it took part in the first military manoeuvres undertaken by the British Army at Chobham in the south of England. During these exercises the 79th was brigaded with the 19th Foot (later The Green Howards) and the 97th Foot (later 2nd Queen's Own Royal West Kent Regiment). As it turned out it was much-needed preparation for the regiment's next period of service as part of the Highland Brigade which proceeded to the Crimea in May 1854.

CHAPTER FOUR

The Crimea and the Indian Mutiny

In the middle of the nineteenth century the people of Britain were forced to confront two crises which struck at the heart of their confidence in the country's armed forces and the whole institution of empire. The first was the war against Russia which was fought in the Crimea and the Baltic, and in which Britain's allies were France, the Ottoman Empire and Sardinia; the second was the Indian Mutiny which broke out in the Ganges valley a year later. Neither was connected in any strategic sense but both rattled the harmony of Victorian life and led to widespread changes in the way the army was organised. All three constituent regiments of the Queen's Own Highlanders took part in the operations in the Crimea and India; the 78th served only in India during the mutiny but it was to gain great distinction by winning eight Victoria Crosses, a new medal for supreme gallantry which was instituted by Queen Victoria in January 1856 to honour 'most conspicuous bravery, or some daring or pre-eminent act of valour or self-sacrifice or extreme devotion to duty' (see Appendix).

The Crimean War encompassed maladministration and

human suffering on a grand scale; disaster marched hand in hand with heroism. It was also the first conflict to be fully covered by the press, most notably by William Howard Russell of *The Times*, and the reports from the front caused national outrage. For the British there was the heroic myth created by Tennyson's well-known poem 'The Charge of the Light Brigade' and the atonement offered by the example of Florence Nightingale and her gallant company of nurses in the infamous military hospital at Scutari. There was, though, more to the war than the oft-rehearsed catalogue of blunders redeemed by basic human courage and a refusal to surrender to overwhelming odds. For all the participants the war ended the long peace of 1815 and set in train the succession of small European conflicts and power struggles which dominated the second half of the nineteenth century, and which would eventually lead to the global war of 1914–18.

The conflict had as its starting point a petty squabble between the Orthodox and Catholic churches over the rights to the holy sites in Jerusalem – the actual spark was possession of the key to the main door of the Church of the Nativity in Bethlehem – and quickly spread to become a war to prevent Russian expansionist ambitions in the Black Sea geo-strategic region. Tsar Nicholas I entertained hopes of using a perceived weakness of Ottoman rule to gain influence in the Balkans, where there was a significant Slav population, and began exerting diplomatic and military pressure on Constantinople. Matters escalated relentlessly and quickly brought the main participants to the verge of war. In the summer of 1853 Russian forces invaded the Ottoman Danubian principalities of Moldavia and Wallachia (modern Romania), a move which forced Turkey to declare war in October. From that point onwards a general conflict became inevitable, as both Britain and France were opposed to the Russian moves and wished to shore up Ottoman rule. At the beginning of 1854 a Turkish naval squadron was overwhelmed and destroyed by the Russian fleet at Sinope, and a few weeks later the British and French fleets sailed into the Black Sea, followed by the mobilisation of both countries' land forces.

War was eventually declared at the beginning of April and command of the British expeditionary force was given to Lord Raglan who, as Lord Fitzroy Somerset, had been Wellington's military secretary in the Peninsula and who had an unblemished, if unspectacular, military career. His connection to Wellington counted for much, as did his personal courage (he lost his right arm at Waterloo) and his ability to get on with the French allies (he spoke fluent French but discommoded these allies in the Crimea by referring to them as 'the enemy').

On the force's departure *The Times* called it 'the finest army that has ever left these shores' but it soon became clear that the encomium was misplaced. No one doubted the courage of the soldiers who went to war with the cheers of their fellow countrymen ringing in their ears, but the direction of the war was soon revealed as a shambles. By the time the British and French forces arrived in the principalities the Russians had withdrawn from the area following an aggressive deployment by the Austrian army. To compound the muddle there was a cholera epidemic in the allied armies and within weeks of landing they had lost 10,000 casualties. With public confidence in the enterprise waning, the decision was taken to attack and destroy the large Russian naval base at Sevastopol on the south-western side of the Crimean peninsula. For the allied armies this meant landing near Eupatoria to the north and attacking down the coastline towards Sevastopol, the idea being to gain the objective before winter set in.

THE CRIMEAN WAR: 72ND AND 79TH HIGHLANDERS

The 79th was part of Raglan's force and left for the Black Sea on 4 May, sailing on board HMS *Simoom*, and landed at Varna within a fortnight. Two months later the regiment moved with the rest of Raglan's army to the Crimea, landing at the ominously named Calamata Bay on 14 November. Together with the 42nd and 93rd Highlanders it formed a Highland Brigade which together with the Guards Brigade made up the Duke of Cambridge's 1st Division. Command of the Highland Brigade had been given to Brigadier-General Colin Campbell, a veteran of the Peninsula and the Sikh Wars in India and one of the few senior British officers who actually cared for and understood his men. The two brigades played a key role in the first set-piece battle of the war on the River Alma on 20 September when the allied and Russian armies collided close to the northern approaches to Sevastopol. The plan of action was the brainchild of the French Marshal Leroy de Saint-Arnaud and left little room for manoeuvre. With both armies drawn up on opposing fronts the French would engage the Russians on the left flank towards the high ground at the river mouth while the British would attack from the centre. If the pincer movement succeeded the Russians would be prevented from withdrawing and their lines of reinforcement and supply would be cut off. It was decided that the French 2nd Division would form the vanguard and advance at five o'clock the next morning followed by the remaining allied divisions two hours later. Covering fire would be provided by the warships lying off the coast.

Dawn the following day brought only confusion and the timetable dictated by the French had to be altered because the British forces were in no position to move off at the agreed hour. However, this was not because of any undue tardiness on the part of the British. Aware that his baggage train and reserve supplies had to be protected, Raglan had ordered part of the army to face east to prevent a possible flank attack and it took time for such a large force to wheel round into the line of march. The growing heat also added to the difficulties faced by the infantrymen, sweating beneath their colourful red or green uniform jackets and the equally exotic headwear of ostrich-feathered caps and rigid shakos.

The delay caused the French to halt – they used the time to brew up mid-morning coffee – and it was not until 10.30 a.m. that the allied army was able to advance on a broad front towards the River Alma. Ahead of them lay a landscape that might have been created for warfare. Taking full advantage of the high narrow escarpment above the winding river, the Russian field commander Prince Menshikov had concentrated his forces on the slopes of Kourgané Hill, which dominated the road to Sevastopol. On the shoulder above the village of Bourliuk two fortified earthworks – known as the Greater and Lesser Redoubts – had been constructed for use by artillery and infantry. This was the centrepiece of the Russian defences: the allies would be obliged to cross the river and press home their attack against well-defended positions on higher ground.

Only to the west had Menshikov left matters to chance but, even so, he clearly thought that his assumptions were correct. Here the escarpment gave way to 350-feet sheer cliff faces flanking the river and so steep and barren were they that Menshikov believed them to be inaccessible. As it was dead ground, only one regiment and a few guns were deployed to guard them, Menshikov having reasoned that no commander in his senses would commit men to a difficult assault against such a precipitous position. Later he claimed not to have known – but should have taken the trouble to discover, given the fact that the Russians were fighting on home ground – that there was a narrow path up the cliff face and that the approaches were by no means impregnable to determined troops. That lack of foresight was to cost the Russians the battle.

But as Menshikov and his staff watched the allied armies halt one mile short of the river they were confident that the expected assault would be stopped in its tracks, secure in the knowledge that they held the high ground and that it would be up to the enemy to dislodge them. Indeed, so carefree was the moment that the Russians had allowed a party of Sevastopol's prominent citizens to take a picnic to the battlefield so that they could watch the expected defeat of the allied forces. From a hastily improvised grandstand on the Telegraph Hill they sat in elegant rows, watching the preparations through opera-glasses and with glasses of champagne within easy reach. At the time watching battles was a common enough practice, no different from spending a day at the races, and the members of the party, which included women, were in high spirits as they watched the two armies square up to one another across the Alma.

It was a moment which none of them, participants or spectators, would ever forget; yet there was an air of unreality about the preparations in the midday heat as the two allied commanders met to confer. What they said is open to doubt, for neither man recorded the conversation, but from what followed it is clear that Raglan rejected Saint-Arnaud's proposal for a flank attack because his cavalry force was outnumbered and therefore he would be unable to dislodge the Russians. Instead, he decided to press home a frontal assault on Kourgané Hill once the French had engaged the Russians on the right. Shortly after 1 p.m. the order to advance was sounded and the first units of the allied army moved forward to cross the river. On the British left was the Light Division, supported by the Duke of Cambridge's 1st Division; to the right was the 2nd followed by the 3rd while the recently arrived 4th Division supplied the reserve together with the cavalry. To their left the French advanced steadily towards Telegraph Hill and started scaling the perpendicular path which Menshikov had unwisely chosen to ignore.

While the French pressed home their attack the British divisions were forced to play a waiting game, Raglan having decided that it would be foolhardy to begin the assault until his allies had made sufficient progress. In any other circumstances it should have been a welcome respite, a quiet moment before battle was joined, but for the patient ranks of infantrymen Raglan's order provided many of them with their first taste of action. While green-tunicked riflemen engaged Russian skirmishers on the riverbanks the Russian artillery on Kourgané Hill fired its first rounds into the unprotected ranks of the 2nd and Light Divisions. Having deployed from column into line, the infantry, drawn up by battalion, made a tempting target and the Russian heavy gunners took advantage of it. According to the historian A.W. Kinglake, who was present and who managed to remain in contact with most of the commanders during this first phase of the battle, the tone was set by Campbell, whose Highland Brigade would attack the heavily defended Russian right. As his men waited under fire and as casualties mounted, he addressed them with 'a few words – words simple, and, for the most part, workmanlike, yet touched with the fire of warlike sentiment':

> Now, men, you are going into action. Remember this: whoever is wounded – I don't care what his rank is – whoever is wounded must lie where he falls till the bandsmen come to attend him. No soldiers must go carrying off wounded men. If any soldier does such a thing, his name shall be stuck up in his parish church. Don't be in a hurry about firing. Your officers will tell you when it is time to open fire. Be steady. Keep silence. Fire low. Now men, the army will watch us; make me proud of the Highland Brigade!

After much dithering, for it was his first experience of battle, the Duke of Cambridge committed the Guards Brigade and the Highland Brigade into action at 3.30 p.m. The attack of the 1st

Division provides the Crimean campaign with one of its many celebrated images. The Guards regiments, the Grenadiers on the right, Scots Fusiliers in the centre and Coldstreamers on the left, advanced with a parade-ground precision which would not have disgraced the Horse Guards; while to their left, on the eastern slopes of Kourgané, the kilted Highlanders pushed ahead with their customary eagerness, anxious to be in a fight. They represented the cream of the British Army, the Guards regiments proud of their discipline and commitment to excellence, the kilted Highlanders jealous of their reputation as fighting soldiers. The battle was won on the slopes of Kourgané Hill, where both brigades attacked the Russian positions with a clinical precision which was graphically described in the 79th's regimental records by Captain Jameson:

> The magnificent mile of line displayed by the Guards and Highlanders, the prominent bear-skin, the undulating waves of clan tartans, the stalwart frames, steady and confident bearing of these young and eager soldiers advancing under fire, can never be forgotten by those who witnessed it, whilst it contributed materially to the discouragement of the enemy, whose columns perceptibly wavered as they approached. His masses of four-and-twenty deep absolutely reeled and staggered to and fro under the murderous fire of the Scottish line, which was delivered with great effect at a distance of 200 yards.

By 4 p.m. the Russian army was in full retreat and the civilian spectators had long since left the battlefield, according to Russell, having been obliged 'to fly for their lives in their carriages'. Menshikov's army was in complete disarray and the first battle to be fought on the European mainland in 39 years was at an end, scarcely three hours after it had commenced in earnest. It was a satisfying moment for Raglan and his first taste of action since he had lost his arm at Waterloo all those years ago. With his staff he left his exposed position and rode over the post road to climb Kourgané Hill to confer with his divisional commanders. At the summit he was greeted by cheering Highlanders, many of whom were meeting their commander for the first time. Carefully averting his eyes from the hill opposite, which was thick with dead and wounded, Raglan thanked Campbell for his work that afternoon. By way of reply the Scottish general asked permission for him and his staff to wear the Highland bonnet in place of the usual cocked hat worn by staff officers, an honour which singled them out from the other brigade commanders. Raglan's eyes filled with tears and he could not speak, but simply nodded his permission. During the fighting the 79th lost two men killed and seven wounded.

The Alma marked the end of the mobile phase of the war. Ahead lay the siege of Sevastopol, which lasted two winters and was destined to take a huge toll in terms of casualties, the majority being victims of disease and illness – of the 367 men of the 79th who died in the war, only nine were killed in action. By then the problems facing the army had become a matter of scandal at home, thanks largely to the exposures published by the *Times* correspondent William Howard Russell, an assiduous reporter of the hardships endured by the soldiers. Some idea of the conditions can be found in the memoirs of Colonel Anthony Sterling, one of Campbell's staff officers in the Highland Brigade:

> All the tents fell in about three minutes; in some the poles broke, in others the pegs drew. As to mine, the wind rushed in at the door, and to split it right up; so my servant and I spent an hour lying on the wet canvas, to keep it compactly down, and to prevent the household goods from being blown away. Just at the first destruction of the tents, the air

was loaded with all sorts of articles – Highland bonnets, shoes, chairs, bits of wood, and all the papers, news or official, in the camp. My box or trunk, which I pillaged, or rather bought from a pillager, to hold my documents, was blown open for a moment, and the wind had just time enough to whip off one document and pour in a shower of water.

All this – and more – was endured by the 79th, which was given some respite the following year when the Highland Brigade, now joined by the 72nd Highlanders, took part in the amphibious operations to take the port of Kertch, which covered the Sea of Azov and was an important conduit for supplying Sevastopol. At dawn on 24 May 1855, 60 ships of the allied fleet made a rendezvous off Cape Takil and following a brief bombardment the troops were able to make an unopposed landing. The town fell quickly and, having destroyed the government buildings and an arsenal, the allies were able to march to Yenikale on the other side of the peninsula. There the destruction continued and it was made worse by the pillaging which followed the order to raze any buildings which might be useful to the Russian war effort. On 9 June the brigade returned to Balaklava and for the rest of the war was involved in the siege operations which led to the fall of Sevastopol on 8 September 1855. As Captain Jameson makes clear, for the Scottish regiments the last few months of the war involved hard and relentless work which often went unsung but was absolutely essential:

> All the available duty men of the Highland Brigade were usually employed at daylight every morning in the severe fatigue of conveying to the army before Sebastopol [sic] round-shot, shell and provisions, the load assigned to each man being generally a 32 lb shot, carried in a sack, or 56 lbs of biscuit. The preparation of gabions and fascines for the

work of the siege, numerous public fatigue duties in the harbour of Balaklava and elsewhere, as well as the labour required for strengthening the entrenchments, likewise devolved upon the brigade.

By the conclusion of hostilities the brigade had expanded to become the Highland Division, following the deployment of 1st and 2nd Royal Scots and the arrival of the 72nd Highlanders. Although the regiments were destined to spend another winter in the Crimea the war was as good as over and diplomacy took over as both sides attempted to broker a peace agreement. The French left first, followed by the British regiments, and each one was met by Queen Victoria who felt that in some small measure she should thank them personally for their loyal services. The 79th landed in Portsmouth in June and the 72nd followed a month later.

THE INDIAN MUTINY: 72ND, 78TH AND 79TH HIGHLANDERS

In the summer of 1857 there was a serious outbreak of violence in India involving Indian regiments of the East India Company's Bengal Army which rapidly escalated to threaten the whole fabric of British rule. On 10 May 1857 the uprising known as the Indian (or Sepoy) Mutiny began at Meerut where the 11th and 20th Native Infantry and 3rd Cavalry regiments rose up against the local European population and started slaughtering them. The trouble had been simmering throughout the year and, amongst other grievances, the flashpoint was the decision to issue Indian troops with cartridges using the grease of pigs and cows, the first being unclean and the second considered sacred. The trouble spread to other British garrisons at Cawnpore where the garrison was slaughtered on 27 June despite promises of safe conduct, and at Lucknow where the European population was besieged in the

Residency by a force of 60,000 mutineers. Reinforcements from Britain were ordered and it was to meet that need that all three regiments were despatched to the subcontinent – the 72nd and 79th from Britain and the 78th from the recent expedition to Persia. All three had different experiences. The 72nd took part in the lesser-known operations in central India while the 78th and the 79th were involved in the fighting in the Ganges plain, which included the famous relief of the garrison at Lucknow.

Having arrived in Calcutta in June 1857 the 78th was soon in action to disarm mutineers at Barrackpore, one of the main cantonments in the Bengal Presidency. From there the battalion moved north to Allahabad, where it joined a relief column under the command of Brigadier-General Henry Havelock, an experienced and well-liked soldier whose career had been hindered by the collapse of his family's fortune and his inability to purchase the necessary promotions. Aged 62 and somewhat old-fashioned in his manner and appearance, he inspired confidence and, more importantly, had a recent success to his credit, having taken part in Outram's expedition to Persia in the previous year. (Not everyone was impressed; one critic described Havelock as 'an old fossil, dug up and only fit to be turned into pipe-clay'.) His orders were clear and to the point: he was to relieve the garrisons at Cawnpore and Lucknow and to 'take prompt measures for dispersing and utterly destroying all mutineers and insurgents'.

Before leaving Allahabad one part of his orders became irrelevant when news arrived that Cawnpore had fallen to the mutineers, but this setback made Havelock more determined than ever to make sure that Lucknow did not meet the same fate. On 7 July his column set out in the teeming rain and heat of the monsoon season; it eventually consisted of 1,403 men comprising a light field artillery battery with eight guns, a portion of 1st Madras Fusiliers, the 64th Foot (later 1st North Staffordshire Regiment) and the 78th Highlanders under the command of Colonel Walter Hamilton. First contact with the mutineers was made on 12 July at Fatehpur where the use of Havelock's nine-pounder artillery pieces proved to be decisive. This was followed by another equally significant action at Aherwa on the Grand Trunk Road, where the 78th was given the task of leading the charge on the rebel positions. This it did with great élan, Havelock noting with approval in his after-action report that 'they cheered and charged with the bayonet, the pipes sounding the pibroch; need I add that the enemy fled, the village was taken and the guns captured?' For the British commander it was a good moment: the opposition had been scattered, during the hottest season of the year his column had marched 126 miles in nine days and Cawnpore was almost in his grasp. As a contemporary account related to the historian W. H. Fitchett reveals, only the heat and dust of the plain prevented a more rapid move towards the beleaguered city:

> It was a march of twenty miles. The sun rose and scorched the silent panting ranks of the British with its pitiless heat. The Highlanders suffered most; they were wholly unprepared for a summer campaign, and were actually wearing the heavy woollen doublets intended for winter use; but their stubborn northern blood sustained them. Every now and again, indeed, some poor fellow in the ranks dropped as though shot through the head, literally killed with the heat. Nana Sahib himself held the approach to Cawnpore with seven thousand troops and a powerful artillery, and his position was found to be of great strength.

What happened next was the defining incident of the mutiny. Having taken Cawnpore the mutineers, led by Nana Govind Dhondu Pant (better known as Nana Sahib), had rounded up the remaining Europeans, mainly women and children, and moved them into a compound known as the Bibighar (ladies' house), where the conditions rapidly deteriorated. Their fate was settled by Havelock's rapid advance: on 16 July Nana Sahib ordered the massacre of the hapless inhabitants of the Bibighar, the resultant death toll being 73 women and 124 children. The following day Havelock's column entered Cawnpore unopposed and made the grim discovery recorded in his diary (held by the National Army Museum) by Major (later General) G. W. P. Bingham, an officer in the 64th:

> The place was literally running ankle-deep in blood, ladies' hair, torn from their heads, was lying about the floor, in scores, torn from them in their exertions to save their lives no doubt; poor little children's shoes lying here and there, gowns and frocks and bonnets belonging to these *poor, poor* creatures scattered everywhere. But to crown all horrors, after they had been killed, and even some alive, were all thrown down a *deep* well in the compound. I looked down and saw them all lying in heaps.

The experience of entering the charnel-house of Cawnpore and descriptions of that kind helped to fuel the desire for revenge and helps to explain the savagery with which the mutiny was put down. In the aftermath of Cawnpore mutineers received little mercy and in subsequent actions British soldiers went into action with the words 'Remember Cawnpore!' ringing in their ears.

Havelock's immediate intention was to push up the Ganges towards Lucknow to relieve the siege before the garrison and their families were butchered, but progress was slow. Not only were the weather conditions against him but the rebels put up stout resistance and by the end of August Havelock had lost 20 per cent of his column to disease or death in action. As a result he was forced to withdraw to Cawnpore to await the arrival of reinforcements under Outram's command. Although senior in rank Outram waived the right to lead the reinforced column, by then 3,000-strong, so that Havelock could complete what he had begun. On 19 September the force set off and two days later the 78th and 90th Light Infantry (later 2nd Cameronians) successfully cleared the village of Mangalwar with a spirited bayonet charge. The 78th lost one killed and six wounded. Despite the onset of heavy rain the advance continued and three days later Lucknow was finally in sight. Havelock ordered that the main assault should be made by the 78th and over two days of heavy fighting (25 and 26 September) the relieving force fought its way into the Residency. In the course of the operations the 78th won a total of six Victoria Crosses, one of which was awarded to them as a regiment, an unusual gesture. Asked to vote on which soldier should receive the award the officers and men selected Assistant Surgeon V.M. McMaster, who had not only tended the wounded under fire but at one stage had carried the Queen's Colour into battle. In his despatch Havelock paid tribute to the 'gallant men and officers' of the 78th who had recaptured the Residency with the support of loyal Indian forces:

> This column pushed on with a desperate gallantry, led by Sir James Outram and myself and staff, through streets of flat-roofed, loop-holed houses, from which a perpetual fire was kept up, and overcoming every obstacle, established itself within the enclosure of the Residency. The joy of the garrison may be more easily conceived than described. But it was not until next evening that the whole of my troops, guns, tumbrels and sick and wounded, continually exposed to the attacks of the enemy, could be brought step by step within the enceinte and the adjacent palace of the Farrah Buksh.

Their efforts came at a heavy price. During the assault phase the attacking column lost 535 casualties, of whom 11 officers and 185 soldiers were killed in action. The 78th's losses were 41 killed and 81 wounded. Worse was to come. Although Havelock's column had managed to get into Lucknow, it had not raised the siege and now found that it too was in peril. Lacking the necessary transport and depleted in size due to the heavy casualties, the relieving force could neither escort the civilians out of Lucknow nor hope to engage the superior numbers of besieging mutineers. In short, the rescuers were now the besieged. To add to the problems, conditions inside Lucknow began to deteriorate, soldiers were put on half rations, their uniforms were in tatters and, according to the regimental records, 'the post of the 78th was all this time exposed by day and night to a ceaseless fire of shot, shell and musketry, and scarcely a day passed in which some casualty did not occur'. A particular menace was the number of mines dug by the Indians besieging the city: 21 shafts were discovered, some them 200 feet in depth.

Fortunately, help was on its way. Fresh from his exploits in the Crimea Lieutenant-General Sir Colin Campbell had been appointed commander-in-chief of the forces in India and had made the relief of Lucknow his priority. On 12 November he arrived at Alam Bagh outside the city with a force of around 700 cavalry and 2,700 infantry and was able to enter the beleaguered Residency a week later. Once again, though, the relieving force was too small to hold the place and Campbell decided to withdraw his forces and establish a new defensive position at the Alam Bagh. The task of forming the rear-guard to cover the withdrawal was given to the 78th. Although the operation was a complete success – the Indian forces besieging the Residency kept up their fire long after Campbell's force had withdrawn – the feat was marred by the loss of Havelock, who succumbed to dysentery and died on 24 November.

The next three months were spent in creating a huge force numbering 25,664 men and consisting of four infantry divisions, one cavalry division, one artillery division and an engineer brigade. Amongst the reinforcement was the 79th, which had arrived in Calcutta in November 1857 and immediately joined Campbell's 3rd Division. By the beginning of March Campbell was ready to attack the mutineers, whose numbers had by then swollen to an estimated 100,000. During the operations the 78th was ordered to secure the Alam Bagh position but the 79th was involved in the 5th Brigade's flanking attack towards the River Gumti, the two other regiments being the 23rd Foot (later The Royal Welch Fusiliers) and the 1st Bengal Fusiliers. The fighting lasted 19 days and involved a good deal of close-quarter fighting before Lucknow was finally recaptured on 21 March. During the operations the 79th lost seven soldiers killed and two officers and 21 soldiers wounded.

Both the 78th and the 79th took part in the remaining operations to subdue Oudh and were involved in an ill-conceived attack on Fort Ruiya under the overall command of Major-General Robert Walpole, who was described by an accompanying army doctor as 'a great dolt'. Even William Howard Russell was not impressed, telling the readers of *The Times* that he was 'surprised Sir Colin [Campbell] trusts his Highlanders to Walpole'. The war reporter's reservations were not misplaced. On entering the rebel stronghold of Rohilkhand from the west of Oudh Walpole approached the fort at Ruiya and, without attempting a preliminary reconnaissance, decided on a frontal assault. He even ignored the intelligence gained by a trooper of Hodson's Horse, an Indian cavalry regiment, that the rebel leader Nirput Singh would retire if a show of force was made in front of the walls. During the attack the defenders were able to produce heavy fire as the first assault troops tried to fight their way towards the steep sides of the mud fort. Altogether Walpole's force lost six officers and 112 soldiers killed or wounded. An officer in the 79th, Ensign (later Major-General) Talbot Glascock, wrote a graphic description of the attack in his diary, which is held in the India Office Library and Records:

> We were kept under the walls of the fort under heavy fire, on the strongest side of the place, nearly the whole day. At last being tired himself, I presume, with doing nothing, the General ordered two companies of the 42nd Highlanders to storm the place alone, while we looked on. Also two companies of a Sikh regiment were sent up but these poor fellows were unable to scale the steep sides of the mud fort, though many tried to fall back into the muddy ditch pursued by many a bullet.

Despite being written off as 'a poor incompetent wretch' by a Sapper officer on his staff Walpole retained Campbell's confidence and there was better fortune for both men when they defeated a rebel force led by Khan Bahadur Khan outside Bareilly on 5 May. This involved fighting in built-up areas – the city consisted of large numbers of sprawling townships and suburbs – and the actual combat was conducted with a ferocity which surprised the attacking force, led by a Highland Brigade consisting of the 42nd, 79th and 93rd Highlanders. The defenders were Muslims and they showed that they were prepared to fight to the death. One account in the records, written by a sergeant, described the 'fanatics, sword in hand with small circular bucklers on the left, and green cummerbund on', rushing out of the defences to engage the Highlanders in close-quarter fighting. Campbell's response was to order the use of the bayonet and Bareilly eventually fell two days later. Although the 78th did not serve in the Highland Brigade at Bareilly, it played a role in the operations, protecting Walpole's heavy guns, which were used to reduce buildings suspected of giving shelter to the mutineers.

Following the successful outcome, the 78th remained in Bareilly as a garrison until 20 February 1859, when it moved to Bombay prior to a return to Britain. For the 79th there was a different fate: the regiment took part in the final operations to secure Oudh, including the relief of Shahjahanpore and the storming of Rampore Kussia, and was destined to remain in India on garrison duty until 1871.

With the fall of Bareilly the mutiny entered its final stages and was officially declared to be over on 8 July 1859. Eighteen months earlier the 72nd had arrived in the country to take part in the operations against mutineers in Central India, serving in the Central India Field Force under Major-General Sir Hugh Rose, another veteran of the war in the Crimea. Their task was to put down a rebellion led by Lakshmi Bai, the beautiful and enigmatic Rani of Jhansi, a Maratha princess who had been forced to give up her state by the East India Company. Spurred on by the events in northern India the previous year she had attempted to reclaim Jhansi with an army commanded by her and Tatya Tope, who had played a leading role in the infamous massacre of Europeans at Cawnpore. At the end of March the 72nd took part in the attack to retake Kotah, a fortified town where the British resident and his family had been murdered. During the assault the regiment was awarded its first Victoria Cross when Lieutenant A.S. Cameron led a small party of men against a strongly defended building and killed three mutineers in close-quarter combat, losing part of his hand in the process. For the rest of the year the 72nd was part of one of the two detachments ordered to pursue the rebels, a task which involved lengthy route marches in hot summer weather. At one stage, during the operations to secure Bhopal, the battalion marched 110 miles in 74 hours, but according to the records the men 'were rewarded by inflicting severe punishment on the mutineers'. The Rani's death in an engagement at Morar near Gwalior effectively ended the rebellion, although mopping-up operations continued into the early part of 1859.

CHAPTER FIVE

High Noon of Empire

The Crimean War and the Indian Mutiny proved to be watersheds in the history of the British Army. In the aftermath of the rebellion in India steps were taken to increase the size of the garrison to ensure that the Indian army of 190,000 soldiers was balanced by the presence of 80,000 British soldiers, an arrangement which meant that between the Crimean War and the First World War the 72nd, the 78th and the 79th all spent much of their time in India, a country which the military historian Correlli Barnett has described as 'the greatest formative influence on the life, language and legend of the British army . . . India, with its heat, stinks and noise, its enveloping dust, became the British army's second home – perhaps its first.' From contemporary accounts it seems to have been an agreeable posting, at least for the officers, who enjoyed a round of 'monthly balls, private parties, amateur theatricals, mess dinners, riding, driving, horse racing etc'. For the rank and file conditions were somewhat different, but the differences in standing between the officers and the men did not make India an unattractive posting. Due to the heat the day began early and parades and inspections were finished by 9 a.m. Those soldiers with wives on the strength generally enjoyed better conditions than they would at home, but for single men time could hang heavily on their hands. Excessive drinking was a problem and so too was venereal disease. In an effort to control its spread, regiments recognised that it was an issue and maintained semi-official brothels, known as 'rags' to the troops, whose inhabitants were inspected by army medical officers.

However, it was the Crimean War which ushered in the biggest changes, since it had exposed gross shortcomings in administration and as a result the War Office instituted a number of reforms to improve the lot of the British soldier. Changes were also made to the operation and structure of the army, but given the prevailing conservatism many of the proposed reforms took time to take root. A Staff College came into being at Camberley to provide further intensive training for promising officers, the Crimean conflict having exposed the weakness of reliance on regimental soldiering alone. Recruitment problems were addressed by introducing short-service enlistment, the number of years being reduced from 21 years to six with the Colours and six in the Reserves. As for the purchase of officers' commissions, which had been much criticised during the war, the system was not abolished until 1871. The reform was welcomed but it had little effect in most infantry and cavalry regiments where the low rates of pay and the high cost of living meant that officers continued to come from the same social background as before – mostly from the upper and professional classes and the landed gentry. On the equipment side the first breech-loading rifles were introduced in 1868 (the Snider followed by the Martini-Henry and the Enfield), but the army's traditional red coats were not replaced by khaki until the 1880s, when campaigning in the deserts of Egypt and Sudan made ceremonial dress inappropriate for operational service. (The change to khaki was gradual and was not made official until 1902.) In appearance the regiments in the Crimea looked remarkably similar to their forebears in the Peninsula.

For the next 60 years Britain was to play no part in the wars which were fought in Europe, the main conflict being the Franco–Prussian War of 1871. Until the outbreak of the Boer War (1899–1902) which brought the century to an end, the army was to spend most of its time engaged in colonial police-keeping duties or counter-insurgency operations in various parts of Britain's imperial holdings.

72ND HIGHLANDERS

Following the Indian Mutiny the 72nd remained in India at Mhow, with detachments at Indore, and in 1865 it moved to Poona for a short time before returning to Britain. Between 1866 and 1871 the regiment was stationed variously at Edinburgh Castle, Aldershot, Manchester and in Ireland. Then it was back to India. Early in 1871 the 72nd arrived in Bombay (now Mumbai) but its posting on this occasion was in the north-west, in stations that are now in Pakistan – Umballa, Peshawar, Nowshera, Cherat and Sialkot. Seven years later the 72nd took part in an operation which restored British prestige in Afghanistan following the disastrous events of 1842 and helped to make the name of one of the greatest soldiers of the Victorian army – Major-General Sir Frederick Sleigh Roberts, immortalised by the poet Rudyard Kipling as 'Bobs', and later a field marshal.

The trouble started during the 1860s, when a series of Russian annexations of neighbouring Tashkent, Samarkand and Khiva made the British believe that their rivals were attempting a pincer movement on the subcontinent. Events reached a climax in 1877 when the emir of Afghanistan, Shere Ali, entertained a Russian delegation but refused to allow a British mission to enter the country. His decision was a severe blow to national pride and the British decided that if Shere Ali would not entertain the presence of a mission he would have one imposed on him. Three field forces were raised for the operation – the Peshawar Valley Field Force under the command of Lieutenant-General Sir Sam Browne, the Kandahar Field Force commanded by Major-General Sir Donald Stewart and Roberts's Kurrum Valley Field Force, which included the 72nd.

During the advance into Afghanistan in November 1878 Roberts's field force encountered the enemy blocking the Peiwar Kotal pass in a seemingly impregnable position. The resulting action made Roberts's name. He directed the 5th Gurkhas with detachments of the 72nd in support on a night march around the left-hand side of the mountainous defile, and they succeeded in outflanking and beating off the Afghans. As a result of the victory a fresh treaty was signed at Gandamuk with the new emir, Yakub Khan, but this proved to be short-lived and Roberts was ordered to continue his advance in Afghanistan. Once again he found his way blocked, this time at Charasiah where the Afghans occupied a mountaintop position. Nothing daunted, Roberts entrusted the assault to the 5th Gurkhas and the 72nd and for the second time they succeeded in outflanking the enemy. It was the last occasion when the regimental colours were carried into action and the resulting victory allowed Roberts's force to enter Kabul before the end of the year. At new year the 72nd and 92nd Highlanders celebrated in the customary way and Roberts joined them for a dram. 'You have always answered when I called on you,' he told them, 'and now I answer your call as readily.'

By the time spring came to the country all appeared to be quiet and to the British it seemed that their regime-change tactics had worked. But the *jihad,* or holy war, continued. In July a British force was annihilated at Maiwand in southern Afghanistan by an Afghan army led by Ayub Khan, Yakub Khan's brother, and the news sent shockwaves through the garrison when it reached Kabul. Out of 2,746 men, 934 had been killed and 175 were wounded.

Then came the news that another force under Major-General Sir James Primrose was besieged in Kandahar. Roberts wasted no time in drawing up a relief force of 10,000 men plus beasts of burden and camp followers, which took 23 days to cover the 350 miles over trackless country in trying physical conditions. On 31 August 1880 the column reached Kandahar to find the garrison so dispirited that they lacked the will to fly the Union flag. Around the city the Afghans were positioned in the high hills and to Roberts's infantry, including the 72nd, fell the responsibility of flushing them out. These last skirmishes ended the Second Afghan War and, having put Abdul Rahman, a nephew of Shere Ali, on the throne, the British were able to withdraw once again from the country.

At the end of the campaign the 72nd returned to India and in November 1880 it moved to Lucknow, where it received news of a change of name. For some time the army had toyed with the idea of creating a territorial system by which regiments would be connected to their own local recruiting area, and initially this linked two regiments in small brigades – in 1873 the 72nd formed 58th Brigade Depot at Stirling with the 91st Highlanders. At the time all regiments numbered 1st to 25th had two battalions, and plans were now prepared to provide all regiments with two battalions through a process of amalgamation. Under this process, which was begun by the Secretary for War, Edward Cardwell, and finalised in 1881 by his successor Hugh Childers, the remaining single-battalion regiments were to be linked with others of their kind to form new two-battalion regiments with territorial designations. Driving the Cardwell/Childers reforms was the theory that one battalion would serve at home while the other was stationed abroad and would receive drafts and reliefs from the home-based battalion to keep it up to strength. As a result of the localisation changes regimental numbers were dropped and territorial names were adopted throughout the army but, as happens in every period of reform, the changes outraged older soldiers, who deplored the loss of cherished numbers and the introduction of what they held to be undignified territorial names, some of which bore no relation to the new regiment's traditions and customs. In this respect the 72nd was fortunate. Despite its early brigade-grouping with the 91st Highlanders, it was eventually amalgamated with the 78th to form The Seaforth Highlanders (Ross-shire Buffs), becoming its 1st battalion. Later in the year, in recognition of the 72nd's earlier history, the title of the new regiment was changed to The Seaforth Highlanders (Ross-shire Buffs, The Duke of Albany's Own).

78TH HIGHLANDERS

On returning to Scotland in 1859 the 78th received widespread public acclaim as the saviours of the Lucknow garrison, and the men were hailed as heroes. For the next four years the regiment was based in England, at Aldershot and Shorncliffe, before moving to Gibraltar, which was to be its home until 1867. Then, as part of the acclimatisation process introduced three decades earlier, the 78th crossed the Atlantic for the first time for a four-year posting to Canada, where it was based initially at Montreal, with a later move to Halifax. In 1871 the regiment returned to Britain to take part in internal security duties in the north of Ireland (1871–73). It was a time of widespread disaffection between the Protestant and Catholic communities. Under the leadership of W.E. Gladstone, the Liberal government had attempted to resolve several outstanding Irish grievances, including the disestablishment of the Church of Ireland, the introduction of a Land Act to protect tenants' rights and the creation of a national university but, far from easing the situation, the proposed reforms heightened tensions between the two communities. During the deployment the 78th was required to provide aid to the civil power to restore order between the two communities. It was a grim foretaste of things to come in Northern Ireland.

For the next six years the 78th remained in Britain, being based variously at Fort George, Aldershot, Dover and Edinburgh. Prior to the introduction of the final stage of the army reforms, the 78th was brigaded with the 71st (Glasgow Highland Light Infantry) in the 55th Brigade, with the depot at Fort George. In many respects it was a logical linking. Both regiments had Mackenzie founders and both wore the Mackenzie tartan, but in the second stage in 1881 these two regiments went their separate ways – the 71st amalgamated with the 74th to form The Highland Light Infantry while, as we have seen, the 78th joined the 72nd to form The Seaforth Highlanders (Ross-shire Buffs, The Duke of Albany's Own), becoming its 2nd battalion. In response to the need to increase the size of the British forces in Afghanistan the 78th was ordered back to India, operating firstly on guarding the lines of communication before moving into Afghanistan to take part in the Battle for Kandahar (see above).

79TH HIGHLANDERS

In the aftermath of the suppression of the uprising in India in 1857–59 the 79th remained in the subcontinent until 1871. It was based in a number of stations including Peshawar, Rawalpindi and Delhi, but despite the advantages of soldiering in India described earlier, the main problem facing the regiment was disease. During its 13 years in the country the 79th lost 336 officers and men to fever. On its return to Britain the regiment was stationed at Parkhurst on the Isle of Wight, where it began a close relationship with the household of Queen Victoria – her residence at Osborne was nearby and the regiment regularly provided Guards of Honour. Before the end of the posting the 79th became a royal regiment, taking the new title of 79th Queen's Own Cameron Highlanders and gaining the right to bear the Royal Badge of Scotland (the Thistle ensigned with the Imperial Crown) on the Regimental Colour. For the rest of the decade the regiment remained in Britain, with postings at

Aldershot, Edinburgh, Fort George and Glasgow before moving to Gibraltar for the period 1879–82.

Under the localisation scheme of 1873 the 79th had been brigaded with the 42nd Royal Highlanders at Perth, where it formed 57th Brigade Depot. One of the first fruits of the new order saw the 79th provide drafts for The Black Watch (as it would soon be known), when it formed part of the expeditionary force sent to the Gold Coast (present-day Ghana) under the command of Major-General Sir Garnet Wolseley to bring law and order to the coastal tribes of West Africa, who were being attacked by an inland tribe, the Ashanti, led by King Kofi Karikari. When the next stage of the Cardwell/ Childers reforms was introduced in 1881 it seemed that the 79th would be paired with the 42nd to become the 2nd battalion of The Black Watch, but as this would have meant exchanging Cameron of Erracht tartan for the official government tartan, the commanding officer Lieutenant-Colonel J.M. Leith wrote to the Adjutant-General explaining that while the regiment had no objection to serving with the 42nd it would not willingly surrender its tartan as it 'would virtually mean the extinction of the 79th Cameron Highlanders as a regiment'. As a result, along with every other regiment in the army, the 79th lost its numbering but it had the distinction of being the only single-battalion regiment in the new Army Reorganisation Scheme. Its title became Queen's Own Cameron Highlanders and its territorial area was designated as Inverness-shire.

1ST, 2ND SEAFORTH HIGHLANDERS

Both battalions of the new regiment began their joint existence in India but the 1st battalion was soon on the move. At the end of 1881 the 1st sailed to Aden, but this was only a prelude to a deployment in Egypt. British involvement in the country had been strengthened by the opening of the Suez Canal in 1869 and the purchase of shares in the operating company six years later, a move which drew Britain into controlling Egypt's internal politics. Obviously, this state of affairs did not appeal to the country's ruler Tewfik Pasha, and the 1880s began with an upsurge of nationalist demonstrations aimed against the British presence. As the situation deteriorated, Britain decided to intervene in the summer of 1882 to restore order after the Egyptian army, led by Colonel Ahmed Arabi, began an internal rebellion. The main army was under Wolseley's command and it consisted of 40,500 troops, at the time the largest expeditionary force sent overseas by the British government. The 1st battalion formed part of a force drawn from the Indian garrison commanded by Major-General Sir Herbert MacPherson VC (late 78th Highlanders) and its task was to cover the flank during the main assault.

Wolseley's tactics to defeat the rebel Egyptian forces led to the Battle of Tel-el-Kebir (see below), in which the insurgents were crushed and order was restored. At the end of the short campaign the 1st battalion returned to England, where it was based at Parkhurst on the Isle of Wight. In 1885 the battalion undertook a tour of public duties at Windsor Castle, and from 1886 to 1897 it was based variously in Edinburgh, Glasgow, Ireland and Aldershot. Its next posting was to Crete in 1897, as part of an occupation force to keep the peace between the Greek population and Turkish militias known as Bashi Bazooks. In the years since the 1st battalion had last served in Egypt there had been a deterioration in the situation in Sudan following the Mahdist revolt (see below) and the creation of an Islamic fundamentalist state overseen by the Mahdi's successor, Abdullah Ibn Muhammed, known as the Khalifa. During his despotic rule those who offended him were subjected to mass murder, rape and savagery and by the 1890s there were calls for him to be deposed and for Sudan to be brought under British–Egyptian rule. The commander entrusted with the task was Major-General Sir Horatio Herbert Kitchener, a Royal Engineer officer with lengthy experience of service in the region.

By 1898 Kitchener had assembled a large and well-trained army consisting of British, Egyptian and Sudanese regiments to complete the process of regime-change by marching on the capital, Khartoum, and defeating the Khalifa's large but poorly equipped 'dervish' forces. The 1st battalion formed part of a British Brigade, which consisted of 1st Royal Warwicks, 1st Lincolns and 1st Camerons. The operation called for meticulous planning to get the 14,000-strong army up the Nile: a railway was constructed, huge quantities of camels were rounded up to provide additional transport and low-draught gunboats accompanied the expedition (one of the naval officers being David Beatty, the future admiral and commander of the British battle-cruisers at Jutland in 1916). The first decisive action took place at the junction of the Nile with the River Atbara, where Kitchener used the British brigade and two Sudanese brigades to attack the dervish encampment which was protected by a *zeriba* or thorn fence. Following a short artillery bombardment at dawn on 8 April, 1st Camerons went into the attack with pipes playing and excited shouts of 'Remember Gordon!' (General Charles Gordon, who had been murdered at Khartoum in 1885.) Behind them came the rest of the British brigade and the 2nd Sudanese Brigade commanded by Hector Macdonald, a Gordon Highlander who had been commissioned from the ranks. Within half an hour it was all over, 3,000 dervishes were dead while the losses in Kitchener's army were minimal: 1st Seaforth lost two officers and six soldiers killed.

The victory allowed Kitchener to be reinforced with a further British brigade and to march on Khartoum, where the decisive battle was fought on 2 September on a bend in the Nile between the hills and the river. The Battle of Omdurman (as it was known) was more of a slaughter than a fight between equals. At first light the Khalifa's army went into the attack chanting 'There is but one God and Mohammad is the messenger of God'. To the waiting British troops this presented an awesome spectacle: line after seemingly impenetrable line of dervishes making their way forward in tight battle order, a wave of humanity pressing forward to break on the concentrated fire of the waiting infantry. However, belief was no armour against the accuracy of British firepower and the battle became a slaughter. Pounded by howitzer shells, mown down by Maxims and a hail of accurate rifle-fire the dervishes, urged on by their emirs, charged to almost certain death. 'They came very fast,' reported G.W. Steevens of the *Daily Mail*, 'and they came very straight, and they presently came no further.' When the smoke cleared some 2,000 dervishes lay dead in front of the British lines; the massacre was almost over and it was 8.30 a.m. The losses in Kitchener's forces were 48 killed. The victory re-established British–Egyptian rule in Sudan and the 1st battalion returned to Cairo where it remained on garrison duty until 1903. Between then and 1914 1st Seaforth was in India where amongst other duties it was involved in operations on the North-West Frontier and took part in the King George's Coronation Durbar in Delhi in 1911.

The 2nd battalion also began its new existence in India, its home until 1897, when it returned to Britain. During that period it saw active service with the Chitral Field Force which was despatched to deal with hostile tribesmen in one of the many disturbances that took place on the North-West Frontier during the nineteenth century. On the battalion's return to Britain it took part in the celebrations to commemorate Queen Victoria's Diamond Jubilee and then headed north back to Scotland for a period at Fort George. It was not destined to enjoy the relative tranquillity of a home posting for long. On 11 October 1899 hostilities broke out with the Boers in South Africa and 2nd Seaforth was ordered to join a new Highland Brigade consisting of 2nd Black Watch, 1st Highland Light Infantry and 1st Argyll and Sutherland Highlanders under the command of Major-General Andrew Wauchope. This proved to be a costly and humiliating conflict not just for the British Army but also, as it turned out, for the Scottish regiments involved.

For most of the nineteenth century Britain had been at loggerheads with the Boers – Dutch immigrants who had settled in Cape Colony – before they started trekking north in 1834 to establish Transvaal and the Orange Free State. However, that did not solve matters and the enmity broke out into open war in 1880 as a result of non-payment of taxes. Following the humiliating defeat of a British force at Majuba Hill an uneasy peace was restored, with the Boers operating self-government under British suzerainty, but it was only a stop-gap arrangement. In 1886 seemingly limitless supplies of gold were discovered in Boer territory south of Pretoria and the promise of untold riches attracted speculators from Britain and all over Europe. Before long the Boers were outnumbered by outsiders who threatened their traditional conservative way of life. To protect the interests of his fellow Boers in the Transvaal President Kruger passed stringent laws excluding non-Boers from participation in political life while retaining the right to tax them.

Such a state of affairs was bound to cause irritation but the British response in 1895 simply caused further trouble. Acting in the mistaken belief that an uprising against the Boers was imminent, the British imperial adventurer Cecil Rhodes encouraged his associate Dr Starr Jameson to lead a raid into the Transvaal to bring down Kruger's government. The so-called 'Jameson Raid' was a fiasco, Rhodes was disgraced, Britain was made a laughing stock and to make matters worse the subsequent negotiations to retrieve the situation settled nothing. Each new concession was met with further demands and gradually war became inevitable. In 1899 Britain despatched 10,000 troops to South Africa to bolster its garrison while the Transvaal, now backed by the Orange Free State, made plans for mobilisation. Within a week of the declaration of war General Sir Redvers Buller VC was on his way to South Africa to take command of the imperial forces in what everyone hoped would be a short sharp war.

The 2nd battalion first saw action on the night of 10–11 December when the Highland Brigade was ordered to engage a Boer position at Magersfontein Kopje ('*kopje*' means 'prominent peak' or 'raised ground') as part of a general advance towards Kimberley, where the garrison was under siege by Boer forces. From the very outset the operation was doomed. Not only was the reconnaissance of the Boer position sketchy and amateurish, but the men of the Highland Brigade had to make a night march to get into position for a dawn attack, always a risky undertaking and doubly so when the lie of the land is unknown. To complicate matters there was a torrential downpour during the night, leaving the men wet and cold as they did not carry greatcoats. Prior to the assault British artillery opened fire on the Boer positions in the heaviest bombardment mounted by the British Army since the siege of Sevastopol over 40 years earlier. To the watching war correspondents it seemed that nothing could have survived such a barrage; they were not to know that the Boers were not on the kopje but had taken up new positions in a long line of trenches which lay below it. Unfortunately these remained undisturbed by the bombardment and this meant that when the Highland Brigade went into the attack the men would be facing sustained and accurate rifle-fire from the hidden Boers.

So it proved. At 4 a.m., as the Highland Brigade column approached the Boer lines with 2nd Black Watch in the lead, Wauchope gave the order to extend the line in preparation for the assault on the Boer positions. As he did so, a heavy fusillade broke out from the Boer trenches and although much of the shooting was initially too high it caused momentary panic and disorder. Thinking to outflank the Boer trenches, Wauchope ordered the line to be extended with the Seaforths and the Argylls to the right of 2nd Black Watch. Although the order was given there was further confusion when Wauchope was killed, and as dawn broke the position of the Highland Brigade was hopeless. With their general dead the command structure collapsed and the brigade was pinned down on the veldt under the hot sun, providing easy prey to Boer snipers. Nine hours later, without food or water and tormented by the scorching sun which burned the back of the men's legs below their kilts, the nerve of the Highland Brigade broke. As it began a panic-stricken retreat to safety the Boer riflemen again took their pick of choice targets; in the fighting at Magersfontein 2nd Seaforth lost 69 killed and 143 wounded.

The news of the disaster caused a tremendous shock when it reached Scotland and the misery was compounded by news of two other heavy defeats at Stormberg and Colenso, a period of setbacks that the war correspondent Arthur Conan Doyle christened 'Black Week'. In an attempt to retrieve the situation the troop levels in South Africa were increased, Buller was sacked and command of the army was given to Lord Roberts. His chief of staff and second-in-command was Kitchener, fresh from his exploits in Sudan, and in the Highland Brigade Wauchope was replaced by Hector Macdonald. The changes lifted spirits and immediately brought results. The new year, 1900, began with the lifting of the siege of Kimberley and in February Kitchener smashed the Boers into submission at Paardeberg in a hard-pounding battle which lasted the better part of a week. During the fighting the four battalions of the Highland Brigade, including 2nd Seaforth, made a frontal attack on the Boer positions and once again they were pinned down by accurate rifle-fire. This time they did not lose their heads but casualties were still heavy – the battalion lost 53 killed and 100 wounded. Paardeberg helped to break the back of Boer resistance and in its aftermath the Highland Brigade came out of the line and was employed on the demanding task of guarding the lines of communication.

This was the turn of the tide and the war entered a new phase, with the invasion of the Orange Free State and the Transvaal. By September Pretoria and Johannesburg had been occupied and the Boer army had capitulated at Brandwater Basin. During this period the 2nd battalion served in the Orange Free State, where life was a mixture of discomfort and boredom interspersed by moments of action against isolated pockets of Boers. To all intents and purposes the war was over. The main Boer strongholds were in British possession, the lines of communication had been secured and the Boer leadership was fractured, but the fighting was destined to last another 18 months in its third and final phase. At the end of the year Roberts handed over command to Kitchener, but instead of tying up the loose ends the new commander-in-chief found himself engaged in a lengthy and bitter guerrilla war with an enemy who refused to give up the fight. As long as they had rifles and ammunition and a sense of loyalty to the Boer cause they saw no reason to surrender; they understood that the numerical superiority of the British Army made outright victory impossible and took heart from the sheer size of their country. Most of the veldt was still free and the guerrillas made it their home, using deception, speed and marksmanship in place of fortification and artillery.

With his army stretched out along the main lines of communication Kitchener decided to turn the position to his own advantage. He began by ordering a series of drives across the country to sweep the Boers out of their hiding places. It was a time-consuming exercise which tried the patience and the endurance of the British Army. Although success was described in shooting terms as 'Boers in the bag' the terrain militated against the methods and huge effort might be rewarded only by a handful of prisoners plus greater numbers of cattle and oxen. For 2nd Seaforth that was their story for the rest of the war, which eventually drew to a close in the spring of 1902 and was concluded by the signing of the

Treaty of Vereeniging. On the battalion's return to Britain it was stationed again in Ireland before a stay at Fort George (1909–11). In 1912 2nd Seaforth moved to Shorncliffe to join 10th Brigade in the 4th Division.

1ST, 2ND QUEEN'S OWN CAMERON HIGHLANDERS

On 7 August 1882 the 1st battalion left for Alexandria on board the troopship *Orontes* and arrived a week later to be joined by 1st Black Watch, 2nd Highland Light Infantry and 1st Gordon Highlanders in the Highland Brigade under the command of Major-General Sir Archibald Alison. They formed part of the force commanded by Wolseley to put down the rebellion led by Colonel Arabi (see above). Ahead of his landing Wolseley let it be known that he intended to make landfall at Aboukir Bay before moving on Alexandria, but that was a ruse. His real destination was Port Said, where he landed his forces on 1 September and at Ismailia took possession of the Suez Canal. From there Wolseley's army moved west, defeating an Egyptian force at Tel-el-Mahuta before concentrating at Kassassin for the assault on the main Egyptian base at Tel-el-Kebir. Arabi thought that his position was impregnable and that the British would be unable to withstand the fierce midday heat to make their expected assault. But having inspected the position Wolseley decided to take part of his force across the desert by night on 12 September, with the Highland Brigade in the vanguard. Naval officers accompanied the infantry columns to navigate by the stars, and before sunlight the following day the force was in sight of the Egyptian defensive positions. The march was described in his memoirs by the battalion's adjutant, Captain K.S. Baynes:

> The weird night march, long to be retained in the annals of the regiment and the country, was a sight never to be

forgotten by those who took part in it; the monotonous tramp, the sombre lines, the dimly discerned sea of desert, faintly lit by the stars, were at once ghostly and impressive. The pace was necessarily slow; one halt was made, and shortly after the directing star having become concealed, another was chosen, and the direction slightly changed to the right.

From their forward position the Highland Brigade went into the attack with Colonel Leith leading the charge, sword drawn and shouting out, 'Come on the 79th!' Their target was formed of high parapets and deep ditches, where the Egyptian soldiers were taken by surprise and stood little chance in the face of the speed and strength of the Highlanders' charge. Inside the defences there was fierce hand-to-hand fighting, which left around 2,000 Egyptian soldiers dead in just under two hours. During the action the 1st battalion's casualties were 17 soldiers killed and 44 officers and soldiers wounded. The victory at Tel-el-Kebir ended Arabi's revolt and with some relief Wolseley was able to send a telegraph to the War Office telling them not to send any more troops to Egypt. However, there was no respite for the 1st battalion, which stayed on as part of the army of occupation. Two years later the battalion was in action again when it formed part of the forces to deal with an Islamic fundamentalist revolt led by Mohammed Ibn Al-Sayd Abdullah. A teacher from Dongola province, he had proclaimed himself the Mahdi, the 'expected one', descendant of the prophet Mohammed, who intended to rid Sudan of infidel forces. To oversee the necessary withdrawal from the area the British government despatched General Charles Gordon to Khartoum where he and his staff were quickly besieged. A relief force set out to save him but it arrived too late – Gordon was murdered on 26 January 1885 – and for the next two years 1st Camerons was stationed on the Sudanese border at Korosko, which is described in the regimental records as 'the name given to a few mud huts lying midway between Asswan and Wadi Haifa'. During this period they saw action against the rebel Sudanese forces defending the force at Kosheh and playing a leading role in fighting in the hills near Giniss.

In 1887 the battalion returned to Britain, where it was based at Devonport before moving north to Scotland. By then its future was in doubt. Recruiting was difficult due to the absence of a second battalion – it had been under strength in Egypt – and in both 1887 and 1892 it was proposed that the regiment should become the 3rd battalion of The Scots Guards. Happily, the idea was rejected, thanks mainly to Queen Victoria's disapproval, and by 1897 the threat disappeared altogether when the regiment was ordered to raise a 2nd battalion as part of the expansion of the infantry. The welcome news reached the regiment during its deployments in Malta (1892–95) and Gibraltar (1895–97) and was a much-needed fillip before 1st Camerons joined Kitchener's forces for the invasion of Sudan (see above). Serving in the same brigade as 1st Seaforth the battalion led the attack into the defensive *zeriba* at the Atbara, the first major battle of the campaign, and it was the Camerons' ferocity and strength of purpose in attack that paved the way for victory. Afterwards Kitchener personally thanked the commanding officer, Colonel G.L.C. Money: 'What your battalion has done is one of the finest feats performed for many years. You ought to be proud of such a regiment.' Five months later 1st Camerons played an equally prominent role in the Battle of Omdurman, which ended the campaign at the beginning of September.

After Kitchener's triumph 1st Camerons returned to Cairo, but it was not the end of the regiment's connection with a general who went on to become the best-known soldier of his generation and the Secretary of State for War in August 1914. Shortly after the battle intelligence reached Kitchener of a party of Europeans at Fashoda upstream of Omdurman. This was a group of French and Senegalese soldiers and officials who had marched into the area from the Congo and seemed to be intent on claiming Sudan for France. Kitchener was ordered to investigate and set off on five river steamers taking with him two Sudanese battalions, a battery of artillery and Maxim guns and E Company 1st Queen's Own Cameron Highlanders. Diplomacy and a show of force permitted an amicable solution, an international incident was avoided and the French commander, Jean-Baptiste Marchand, withdrew – the British prime minister, Salisbury, described him discreetly as 'an explorer in distress'. From the Sudan campaign onwards the Camerons had a high place in Kitchener's affections. In the forthcoming war in South Africa they furnished his headquarters guard and they supplied a guard of honour when he returned to Southampton in triumph in June 1902.

At the beginning of the new century 1st Camerons left Cairo as part of the general reinforcement in South Africa following the disasters of 'Black Week'. Serving in 21st Infantry Brigade the battalion took part in the advance to Pretoria and was present at Diamond Hill, fought on 11–12 June and one of the last set-piece battles of the war. During the sweeping-up operations the battalion was based in the Orange Free State and Transvaal. The regiment's first Victoria Cross was won by Sergeant Donald Farmer (see Appendix), who served in 1st Camerons Mounted Infantry Company. These formations had been ordered by the War Office as 'a matter of immediate urgency and permanent importance' and their members were supposed to 'shoot as well as possible and ride decently'. Acting as scouts and as rapid-response forces they were to be one of the more successful innovations of the war.

On the conclusion of the war in South Africa 1st Camerons returned to Britain to be based at Fort George (1902–04), Ireland (1907–07), Tidworth and Aldershot (1907–13) before moving to Edinburgh Castle. By then the 2nd battalion had come into being on 1 April 1897 and it quickly settled into the rhythms of life as a regular infantry battalion in the British Army. Between 1899 and 1903 it provided the garrison in Gibraltar before moving to South Africa on internal security duties. China was the next station and in 1909 2nd Camerons moved to India to become part of 81st Brigade in 27th Division at Poona.

CHAPTER SIX

The First World War 1914–16

During the summer of 1914 a series of events in Europe plunged the world into a conflict which involved all the major powers, including Britain. The flashpoint was provided by the assassination of the Archduke Franz Ferdinand, heir to the throne of Austria-Hungary, who was killed with his wife while visiting Sarajevo, the capital of Bosnia-Herzegovina, in June. At first the news made little impact in Britain and initial reports suggested that the perpetrators would be apprehended and punished, but when it became clear that neighbouring Serbia might have been implicated in the attack the crisis deepened. On 23 July, weeks after the assassination, Austria-Hungary issued an ultimatum to Serbia, making ten demands for the suppression of Serb nationalist groups, the punishment of the assassins and participation in the judicial process. Serbia was given 48 hours to comply and although its response was placatory its government stopped short of allowing Austria-Hungary to take part in the trial of the assassins, arguing that the matter should be referred to the International Court at The Hague. That readiness to cooperate seemed sufficient to settle the problem but already diplomacy was proving powerless to stop Europe's drift towards war. Both countries mobilised their armed forces when Germany, Austria-Hungary's main ally, encouraged Vienna to take decisive action against the Serbs before any other country intervened in the crisis. Confident of German support Austria-Hungary declared war on Serbia five days after issuing its first demands, thus paving the way for a wider conflict. The following day, 29 July, Russia, Serbia's traditional friend and protector, began to deploy its forces along the border with Austria and within 24 hours this was followed by the order for full mobilisation.

Although the move was made to discourage Austria it threatened Germany, which immediately demanded that Russia 'cease every war measure against us and Austria-Hungary'. On 1 August Germany declared war on Russia, followed two days later by a further declaration of war against France, Russia's ally. That same day German forces began crossing into Belgium as part of the prearranged Schlieffen Plan, to bypass the heavily fortified French frontier and encircle Paris from the north through Belgium. Britain, which had wanted to remain aloof from the crisis and was not formally in alliance with any of the main participants, was now about to be pressed into the conflict through a treaty of 1839 which guaranteed Belgium's neutrality. On 4 August, no answer having been received to an ultimatum that Belgium should remain unmolested, Britain declared war on Germany. As part of the 'Precautionary Period' of the Defence Plan Prior to Mobilisation, formations of the Regular Army based in Britain were told to return to their depots on 29 July. Most were on their annual summer camps or undergoing live firing exercises. At the outbreak of war 1st Seaforth was based in Agra (7th Meerut Division) while the 2nd battalion formed part of 10th Brigade, 4th Division at Shorncliffe. The 1st Queen's Own Cameron Highlanders was one of three regiments based in Scotland, at Edinburgh Castle, while the 2nd battalion was in Poona in India. Later it would serve with 81st Brigade, 27th Division. The British-based battalions crossed over to France with the first elements of the British Expeditionary Force (BEF) in the third week of August while the overseas-based battalions arrived in France from September onwards.

At the outbreak of war Field Marshal Lord Kitchener (as the victor of Omdurman had become) was appointed Secretary for War and at his first Cabinet meeting he astonished his colleagues by claiming that the war would last three years and would require over one million men to win it. On 8 August the call went out for the 100,000 volunteers who would form the first of the New Armies. Kitchener's methods were also controversial. Instead of expanding the part-time soldiers of the Territorial Force which had been raised for home defence in 1908 he decided to build on the existing regimental structure of the British Regular Army. No new formations would be raised but the existing infantry regiments would expand their numbers of battalions to meet the demand for men. These would be known as 'special service battalions' and the men who joined them would volunteer for the duration of the war. In that way, argued Kitchener, the volunteers could be assimilated quickly into the 'New' or 'Kitchener' armies and no new machinery would have to be assembled to deal with them. Although Kitchener placed little faith in the soldiers of the Territorial Force, dismissing them as a 'town clerk's army' full of sky-larkers, the existing battalions were allowed to volunteer for service overseas. Once introduced, on 13 August, the idea caught on and group pressure made it difficult for serving Territorials to refuse to serve overseas if most of the battalion volunteered. All the first-line Territorial battalions of The Seaforth Highlanders and Queen's Own Cameron Highlanders served abroad, on the Western Front and in Gallipoli, Palestine, Mesopotamia and Salonika.

During the period 1914–19, the two constituent regiments of the Queen's Own Highlanders expanded considerably to produce the following Regular, Territorial and Special Service battalions:

The Seaforth Highlanders

1st Battalion (Regular Army), Agra, India, 19th (Dehra Dun) Brigade, 7th (Meerut) Division

2nd Battalion (Regular Army), Shorncliffe, Kent, 10th Brigade, 4th Division

3rd (Reserve) Battalion (Regular Army), Cromarty

1/4th (Ross Highland) Battalion (Territorial Force), Dingwall

2/4th (Ross Highland) Battalion (Territorial Force), Dingwall

3/4th (Ross Highland) Battalion (Territorial Force), Dingwall

1/5th (Sutherland and Caithness) Battalion (Territorial Force), Golspie

2/5th (Sutherland and Caithness) Battalion (Territorial Force), Golspie

3/5th (Sutherland and Caithness) Battalion (Territorial Force), Golspie

1/6th (Morayshire) Battalion (Territorial Force), Elgin

2/6th (Morayshire) Battalion (Territorial Force), Elgin

3/6th (Morayshire) Battalion (Territorial Force), Elgin

7th (Service) Battalion (New Army), Fort George

8th (Service) Battalion (New Army), Fort George

9th (Service) Battalion (New Army), Fort George

10th (Reserve) Battalion (New Army), Cromarty

1st Garrison Battalion (New Army), Tillicoultry (1916)

Queen's Own Cameron Highlanders

1st Battalion (Regular Army), Edinburgh Castle, later 1st Brigade, 1st Division

2nd Battalion (Regular Army), Poona, India, 81st Brigade, 27th Division

3rd (Reserve) Battalion (Regular Army), Inverness

1/4th Battalion (Territorial Force), Inverness

2/4th Battalion (Territorial Force), Inverness

3/4th Battalion (Territorial Force), Inverness

5th (Service) Battalion (New Army), Inverness

6th (Service) Battalion (New Army), Inverness

7th (Service) Battalion (New Army), Inverness

8th (Reserve) Battalion (New Army), Invergordon

9th (Labour) Battalion (New Army), Blairgowrie (1916)

10th (Lovat Scouts) Battalion (Territorial Force), Cairo (1916)

11th (Service) Battalion (New Army), Etaples, France (1918)

1st (Home Service) Garrison Battalion (New Army), Invergordon

The expansion of the British Army during the First World War is an example of improvisation and enthusiasm to meet a common cause and the army's family of regiments expanded rapidly as a result. Willing recruits in Inverness rushed to join a special service battalion of Queen's Own Cameron Highlanders that was being formed by D.W. Cameron of Lochiel, who published an appeal for volunteers from 'any young man of Highland birth or parentage, of good physique and having good teeth, between the ages of 19 and 30, who wishes to serve under me in the defence of his country and for the rights of liberty and against military oppression'. It would fight as the 5th Camerons and Lochiel offered his personal guarantee that 'at the end of the war the battalion would be brought back to Inverness where it will be disbanded with all possible despatch'.

A number of factors prompted those volunteers from all over Scotland to take the king's shilling. Workers doing repetitive or menial jobs saw a chance to escape the drudgery of their existence.

The Scots' inherent respect for militarism also encouraged many a young man who thought he would look a god in a kilt and a Glengarry bonnet. Others, like Carson Stewart, simply let curiosity get the better of them: in September he went down to the Institute in Cambuslang to watch the crowds of young men queuing to join up and was so enthused by the sight that he joined up himself and was 'duly sworn in and became a soldier of the king in the Queen's Own Cameron Highlanders'. The newly enlisted Private Stewart had joined the regiment's 7th (Service) Battalion, which would serve with the 15th (Scottish) Division in the Second New Army.

From Cambuslang he went north to the regiment's depot in Inverness, where a Camerons' officer remembered that conditions were not always of the best: 'Soon the barracks were crowded out, and for a few nights men had to sleep where they could. Even the distillery at Inverness (already with an insect population of its own) was brought into use.' In the first flush of enthusiasm the War Office's problem was not to raise sufficient recruits so much as what to do with them once they had enlisted. So great was the pressure on the existing army structure that recruits frequently went without uniforms, weapons with which to train and even accommodation. Vast tented encampments soon mushroomed in civic parks, farmers' fields and country estates as enthusiastic recruits drilled with broomsticks while still wearing their best suits. To meet the shortages, production of khaki uniforms and boots had to be increased, supplies were purchased from the United States and the Post Office helped out with blue uniforms surplus to requirement. Stewart and his fellow Cameron volunteers did not feel that they were proper soldiers until the first kilts were issued later in the year.

THE WESTERN FRONT
The Seaforth Highlanders, 1st, 2nd, 1/4th, 1/5th, 1/6th, 7th, 8th, 9th battalions

Shortly after the outbreak of hostilities 2nd Seaforth crossed over to France as part of the deployment of the BEF and was soon in action at Le Cateau on 26 August. It was the British Army's biggest set-piece battle since Waterloo and their 55,000 soldiers faced German opposition which numbered 140,000. Three divisions, led by Lieutenant-General Sir Horace Smith-Dorrien, GOC II Corps, and supported by the Cavalry Division, were able to hold the line by dint of their superior firepower but by evening they were outnumbered and only a German failure to press home their advantage allowed II Corps to resume its retreat. Even so, the casualties were heavy – 7,812 killed – and gave a stark indication of worse things to come. Exhausted by the battle and the summer heat the BEF continued to pull back amid rumours that the war was lost and that the French government had evacuated Paris for Bordeaux. The retreat to Mons was halted on the Marne by mid-September and this new phase of the operations signalled the end of a war of manoeuvre as both sides struggled to fill the gap between the Aisne and the Channel coast before it was exploited. This was known as the 'Race for the Sea' and it ended in stalemate, with the only gap in the line being the wastes of the Flanders plain, an unprepossessing region peppered with names which soon became drearily familiar to the soldiers who fought over it – Ypres, Passchendaele, Messine, Langemarck, Vimy, Arras. The style of the fighting was also changing as the armies faced one another in the fields of Flanders. Trenches were dug, barbed-wire obstacles were thrown up and field fortifications constructed; the German plan to encircle Paris had finally been blunted in the mud of Flanders and the first great set-piece battles were about to be fought.

Before winter set in 1st Seaforth arrived in France from India to take up positions in the front line north of La Bassée, where it was brigaded with 1/4th Seaforth which had arrived in France on 4 November – one of the first Territorial Force formations to be sent into the front line. Both battalions saw action in the first battles of 1915 at Aubers Ridge and Neuve Chapelle. In this spring offensive the British and the French attacked in Flanders and Artois, the French alone in the Champagne. For the British this involved them in battles at Neuve Chapelle, Aubers Ridge and Festubert, and later in the year at Loos. All failed to achieve the Allies' objectives and all produced large numbers of casualties. The first battle, Neuve Chapelle, was initiated by Field Marshal Sir John French, the commander of the BEF, to win back a German salient captured in October 1914. This position gave the Germans the freedom to fire on British positions from both flanks and the danger had to be eliminated but French also hoped to exploit any success by threatening the German lines of communication between La Bassée and Lille. The British field marshal was also anxious to demonstrate to his doubting French allies that his forces had retained their offensive capability and had a significant role to play in the war. By then the British military presence in France and Flanders had expanded and the attack would be made by formations of the British First Army under the direction of General Sir Douglas Haig – IV Corps (7th Division, 8th Division and the Lahore and Meerut divisions of the Indian Corps, in which 1st and 1/4th Seaforth Highlanders were serving). Neuve Chapelle provided other 'firsts'. It was the first battle of the trench system, it was the first to involve Indian troops – the Garwhal and Bareilly brigades of 7th (Meerut) Division attacked on the right – and it was the first to use new artillery tactics, with the British guns firing in support of the infantry.

The plan was to attack on a narrow front of only 2,000 yards using four infantry brigades in the initial assault phase. When the battle was finally called off, on 14 March, the losses on both sides were high – the British lost 11,652 casualties killed, wounded or taken prisoner and the Germans an estimated 8,500. The Seaforth casualties were so high that both battalions were held in reserve during the Battle of Festubert in June when the 1/5th and 1/6th battalions first saw action fighting with the 51st (Highland) Division. The regiment's three New Army battalions, 7th, 8th and 9th, arrived in France by the early summer of 1915 and all saw service in the Battle of Loos, which began on 25 September and which resulted in heavy casualties (see below).

Queen's Own Cameron Highlanders, 1st, 2nd, 1/4th, 5th, 6th, 7th battalions

Both the regular battalions of Queen's Own Highlanders took part in the opening phase of the offensive operations in France and Flanders in 1914. The 1st battalion also took part in the unsuccessful attack on German positions at Aubers Ridge while the 2nd battalion fought in the Second Battle of Ypres to defend the Ypres salient in April 1915. By then 1/4th Camerons had also seen action at Neuve Chapelle and Festubert and the three New Army battalions, 5th, 6th and 7th, had all arrived in France in time to take part in the Battle of Loos, which involved two Scottish New Army divisions, 9th and 15th. For all of Scotland it was a defining moment in the country's experience of fighting on the Western Front: of the 72 battalions in the six attacking divisions, half their number were Scottish, making it the largest concentration of Scottish soldiers on a battlefield since Culloden in 1746. The casualties were proportionally high too. On the second day, at Hill 70, the Scottish battalions were pinned down on the forward slopes by German machine-gun fire and were forced to dig in. At nightfall 6th Camerons made a determined but suicidal bid to drive the Germans off the hill. John Jackson, a volunteer from Glasgow who had enlisted the previous year, recorded the epic struggle in his diary:

The situation was serious, and anxiously we looked back for reinforcements but no help could we see. A third time we charged on that awful hillside, but the enemy with his reserves at hand, were too many for us and again we fell back. Truly we were holding to the motto of the regiment 'A Cameron never can yield'. [This is in fact part of the chorus of 'The March of the Cameron Men', composed in 1829.] We numbered at this stage less than 100 all told, and for all we knew might be all that was left of 6th Camerons. As the evening drew on we made a fourth and final attempt to win and hold the ridge. This time we meant to do or die. Led by our brave old colonel, bareheaded and with no other weapon than his walking stick, we made for the top of Hill 70 through murderous rifle and machine-gun fire, while shells crashed all around us. Our action was a sort of last desperate chance, but in the face of such heavy odds it could only end in failure. The white-haired old man who led us was shot dead, and shortly afterwards Capt. Milne, cool and unruffled to the last, paid a similar penalty.

Jackson's commanding officer, the 'white-haired old man', was Lieutenant-Colonel Angus Douglas-Hamilton and Captain Milne was the battalion's adjutant. For his bravery and leadership under fire Douglas-Hamilton was awarded the Victoria Cross posthumously, one of five to be awarded to Scots after the battle. The following day, 27 September, Corporal James Dalgleish Pollock, 5th Camerons, showed equally cool courage by holding up a German attack from the Hohenzollern Redoubt. By a coincidence, Pollock's cousin, Corporal James Lennox Dawson, 187th Field Company Royal Engineers, was also given the highest award for gallantry after firing bullets into three leaking gas cylinders and saving many men from being gassed during a British attack.

Now was the time to deploy the reserves but it was at this point that the British plan began to unravel. French put the three reserve divisions – Guards, 21st and 24th (the latter two both inexperienced New Army divisions) – under Haig's command, but it took time for them to make their way to the front and by the time they assembled between Loos and the Hulluch–Vermelles road on the morning of 26 September, they were tired and hungry. Overcrowding in the rear of the British line had added to their difficulties, the roads were heavily congested and in some sectors units were forced to bypass British obstacles, compounding the confusion. At the same time the Germans had been busy reinforcing their own positions and by the time the two reserve New Army divisions began their attack they were met with sustained machine-gun and artillery fire. Later, German regimental historians recorded the amazement of their gunners as they saw the serried lines of British infantrymen marching relentlessly towards them, offering targets which could not be missed. Although the attack battalions continued their advance with great gallantry and determination the men were doomed and by nightfall those who had not been killed were either in retreat or were pinned down under the inexorable German fire. So great was the slaughter that the German gunners showed compassion and eventually held their fire as the survivors began the long retreat. Total disaster was avoided when the Guards Division stabilised the situation and the Germans, too, were in no position to counter-attack decisively, but by nightfall on 27 September any hope of a successful 'Big Push' had evaporated.

At the end of the month the French attack in Champagne was brought to a standstill, and coupled with the failure at Vimy, the Allied autumn offensive achieved little in return for huge losses. Bowing to the demands of the French, Haig kept the battle going in the British sector until 16 October, by which time the British casualties at Loos and the subsidiary attacks amounted to

2,466 officers and 59,247 other ranks, killed, wounded or missing. Assessing the actual number of deaths is difficult. Regimental War Diaries tabulated the casualties after the battle but the number listed as 'killed' invariably increased in the aftermath as men died of their wounds and those listed as 'missing' were found to be dead. Even so, the casualty figures at Loos were high and for the Scots they were even higher. Jackson recorded that of the 950 men of the 6th Camerons who had gone into action 700 had become casualties; at the roll-call the survivors simply called out 'over the hill' when the name of a missing man was read out. Some idea of the losses can be seen from the official figures, which show that 6th Camerons and 7th Seaforth were amongst seven Scottish infantry battalions which lost their commanding officer, and of the 12 British battalions which lost more than 500 casualties, two of them were 7th Camerons (687) and 8th Seaforth (502).

GALLIPOLI
1st, 2nd Lovat Scouts, 10th (Lovat Scouts) Battalion, Queen's Own Highlanders

The Lovat Scouts had been raised in 1900 to serve as reconnaissance troops in South Africa and provided two yeomanry regiments in the period before the First World War, taking their recruits from the same Highland counties as the Camerons. At the outset of hostilities both the 1st and 2nd Lovat Scouts were mobilised at Beaufort and travelled south to join the Highland Mounted Brigade at Huntingdon. Both were despatched to Gallipoli in September 1915 in the dismounted role to support the operations being undertaken by a joint British–French expeditionary force to engage the forces of the Ottoman Empire in one of the most ill-starred operations of the First World War. The stalemate on the Western Front had encouraged the idea of opening a second front and the opportunity was provided by Turkey's entry into the war in December 1914. The original plan was to take

Constantinople, capital of the Ottoman Empire, which would be attacked through the Dardanelles to allow a joint British and French fleet to enter the Black Sea following the destruction of the Turkish forts on the Gallipoli peninsula. At that point it would be safe to land ground forces to complete the capture of the peninsula and to neutralise the Turkish garrison. Unfortunately, the operation did not work out that way. Following the failure of the naval operations to destroy the Turkish forts it was decided to land troops at Cape Helles on 25 April but the landings were opposed by the Turks, who offered stout resistance, and by the end of the month the British had suffered around 9,000 casualties, one-third the size of the attacking force. Reinforcements were required and amongst them was part of 52nd (Lowland) Division, which began landing in the peninsula in the first week of June. Its men were in action in the first major offensive at Helles on 28 June, which continued into the following month and caused huge numbers of casualties in the assault battalions.

The men of The Lovat Scouts soon found that they were facing conditions which were as bad as anything on the Western Front. Not only was the fighting conducted at close quarters, with some trenches being almost in touching distance, but the physical hardships were horrendous. Despite the best efforts at maintaining basic sanitation disease was rampant, especially dysentery and enteric fever, which was spread by the absence of proper latrines and washing facilities and by the ever-present swarms of black, buzzing flies. One medical officer said it was impossible to eat in their presence as they quickly swarmed onto any spoonful between plate and mouth.

In October the inevitable happened: the senior British commander, General Sir Ian Hamilton, was sacked, rightly so as his leadership had become increasingly feeble and sterile, and he was replaced by General Sir Charles Monro, a veteran of the fighting on the Western Front. Having taken stock of the situation he recommended evacuation, although this was not accepted until the beginning of November when Kitchener himself visited the battle-front and found himself agreeing that the difficulties were insuperable. A heavy and unexpected winter storm also helped to decide the issue – over 280 British soldiers died of exposure, including a number from the Worcestershire Regiment, who were found frozen to death on the fire steps of their trenches.

In a brilliant operation, which was all the more inspired after the fiascos which preceded it, the British finally withdrew their forces at the end of 1915, remarkably without losing any casualties. The failure of the campaign left a lasting bitterness amongst those who had taken part, not least in Australia and New Zealand, where 25 April is still commemorated as Anzac Day. Unlike the Western Front, where optimism survived for a surprisingly long time, there were no good words to be said about Gallipoli and soldiers who served on both fronts admitted that the conditions on the peninsula were worse than anything they encountered in France and Flanders. Very few of the men who fought at Cape Helles or Suvla would have disagreed with the words of Lord Lovat, who commanded the Highland Mounted Brigade: 'It will be up to date and probably to all eternity, as sordid and miserable a chapter of amateur enterprise as ever was written in our history.' Following the withdrawal from Gallipoli the two Lovat Scout battalions were amalgamated to form the 10th (Lovat Scouts) Battalion, Queen's Own Cameron Highlanders, and subsequently saw service in Salonika (see Chapter Seven).

MESOPOTAMIA
The Seaforth Highlanders, 1st battalion

When it became clear that Turkey was going to enter the war on the side of the Central Powers in the late summer of 1914 the British government authorised the despatch of an Indian Expeditionary Force ('Force D'), consisting of three infantry brigades, to proceed to the Ottoman province of Mesopotamia (present-day Iraq) to safeguard the oilfields and refineries of the Anglo-Persian Oil Company at Ahwaz. The force landed near the mouth of the Shatt-al-Arab waterway, and by the end of November it had secured the city of Basra and the surrounding area, having defeated Turkish forces in a number of small but fiercely contested engagements. All the objectives had been achieved – access to the Persian Gulf had been secured and local Turkish resistance had been neutralised. Even when the Turks counter-attacked at the beginning of 1915 they were repulsed with heavy losses, and this success encouraged thoughts of pressing the attack up the River Tigris to take Baghdad. For the Allies this was a tempting prospect, for although there was no strategic need to make an immediate move, the capture of such an important city would do wonders for Western prestige following the setbacks at Gallipoli. From a military point of view it also made sense, as the nearest Turkish reserves were believed to be at Aleppo in present-day Syria or fighting the Russians in the Caucasus. None were thought to be within 400 miles of Baghdad. Command of the Mesopotamian forces was given to Lieutenant-General Sir John Nixon and he was later reinforced with two Indian divisions from France – 3rd (Lahore) and 7th Meerut. Serving with them were three Scottish battalions – 2nd Black Watch, 2nd Seaforth Highlanders, 1st Highland Light Infantry – which had been withdrawn from the fighting on the Western Front in December 1915.

All three took part in the operation which has come to symbolise the failings of the campaign in Mesopotamia – the relief of the forces besieged in the town of Kut-al-Amara. This came about as a direct result of the move to take Baghdad, which began in May with a move up the Tigris by a mixed British–Indian force commanded by Major-General Charles Townshend, an experienced if somewhat arrogant Indian Army officer. From the outset the odds were stacked against him, as the advance would overstretch his lines of communication and he was operating during the intense heat of summer, but Townshend made good progress with his 14,000-strong ground force backed by a number of gunboats. The town of Al-Amarah fell on 3 June, allowing him to move up the eastern bank of the Tigris towards Kut-al-Amara, which was captured on 28 September. However, even at that stage Townshend's forces were already running into problems. He was almost 400 miles north of his base at Basra and, although he did not know this, the Turks would soon be reinforcing their Mesopotamian garrison with forces from the Gallipoli front. Townshend was cautious about continuing the operation but Nixon was enthusiastic and the first signs were encouraging. Continuing his approach on the west bank of the river Townshend defeated a Turkish force at Aziziye and by 12 November he was within 30 miles of Baghdad. Ahead lay a heavily fortified Turkish position at Ctesiphon which was manned by 30,000 soldiers backed up by German advisers. Townshend's force was half that number but on 22 November his forces attacked and seized the Turks' first lines. That was the only success: the Turks rushed reserves into the area and after three days of fighting Townshend's force had lost 4,511 casualties, killed or wounded. Forced to retreat, the rump of the force reached Kut-al-Amara on 3 December and began preparing for a lengthy siege.

Military logic suggested that Townshend should have continued his retreat but he shared Nixon's confidence that the relief force would arrive before the position became untenable. Perhaps he was too sure of his abilities. In 1895 Townshend had come to prominence as the 'Hero of Chitral', having weathered a 46-day siege surrounded by hostile tribal forces in the north-west Indian town of Chitral while serving as a captain in the 2nd Central Indian Horse. (This operation had involved 2nd Seaforth.) It was only natural that he believed that it was possible to repeat the experience in Mesopotamia. Kut (as it is commonly called) was situated in a loop in the Tigris and although that feature added to the position's defensive properties it also made it easy to besiege. Having failed to break into Kut, two Turkish divisions began the investment and within a week of Townshend's arrival they had completed their blockade. According to the German commander of the Turkish Sixth Army, General Colmar von der Goltz, the British had been 'bottled with the cork in'; they could neither escape nor take in fresh supplies. Inevitably, conditions began to deteriorate inside Kut, which was little more than a collection of mud huts and compounds, and life for Townshend's force soon became intolerable. Sanitation was a problem and because some positions were below the water level it proved difficult to build trenches to protect the men from constant Turkish attack. Supplies began running out and by the beginning of March the average daily ration was ten ounces of barley flour and four ounces of barley grain. Horse and mule meat was also available, although this was usually refused by the Indian soldiers.

With the arrival from France of the two Indian Army divisions the first attempts were made to relieve Townshend's force, but from the outset it was clear that this would not be the easy operation forecast by Nixon. The winter rains made the going difficult, the supply lines were no better than they had been for the first operation and the Turks had been able to reinforce in strength and had occupied strong defensive positions. Haste also played a part. The forces were despatched north as soon as they arrived in Basra, often without their horses, supply wagons and ambulances, and the commander of the operation, Lieutenant-General Sir Fenton Aylmer, had no clear idea of how he should proceed. The result was one disaster after another. The first attack took place on 7 January against heavily defended Turkish positions at Shaikh Saad, where the British and Indian infantry battalions attacked without artillery or cavalry support.

Under the command of Lieutenant-Colonel W.M. Thomson, 1st Seaforth had suffered equally high casualties, being reduced at one stage to fewer than 100 able-bodied men, and as a result the survivors from the battalion were grouped with 2nd Black Watch as a composite Highland Battalion, which was involved in the next stage of the operations at Sannaiyat. This took the relieving force 12 miles short of Kut, but despite the gallantry shown by the British and Indian soldiers the attempt to relieve Kut ended in failure when Townshend was forced to surrender on 27 April. The siege, the longest in British military history, had lasted 147 days and had cost over 2,500 casualties dead and wounded. For those who survived, though, the future was bleak. Put into Turkish captivity and marched north under deplorable conditions, only 837 of the 2,592 British soldiers survived the war, while of the 10,486 Indian and Gurkha soldiers 7,423 survived.

Coming on top of the debacle at Gallipoli in the summer of 1915, when an Allied attempt to knock Turkey out of the war failed following a naval attack on the Dardanelles and subsequent landings on the Gallipoli peninsula, the surrender at Kut was a serious blow to British morale in the Middle East. Not only had neither campaign done anything to shorten the war or discomfit the enemy, but they had been expensive in terms of personnel and equipment. The defeats had also damaged British prestige and it was clear that much-needed stability had to be brought to the British and Indian forces in Mesopotamia. Command was given to Major-General Sir Frederick Stanley Maude, a veteran of the Western Front who spent the rest of 1916 consolidating his forces before taking the attack back to the Turks.

SALONIKA
Queen's Own Cameron Highlanders, 2nd battalion

The withdrawal from Gallipoli allowed the British and the French to build up forces in the Balkans, both to support Serbia and to prevent Bulgarian forces from influencing events in the region –

Kenneth Mackenzie, Earl of Seaforth, who raised the 78th (later 72nd) Highlanders in 1778. From a portrait by H.D. Hamilton.

Francis Humberston Mackenzie, Lord Seaforth, who raised the 78th Highlanders in 1793. Copy by William Dyce of the portrait by Sir Thomas Lawrence PRA.

Lieutenant-General Sir Alan Cameron of Erracht, who raised the 79th Cameron Highlanders in 1793. Portrait by an unknown artist.

Piper Kenneth Mackay, 79th Cameron
Highlanders, at the Battle of Waterloo, 1815.
Painting by Lockhart Bogle.

The 79th Cameron Highlanders at the Battle of the River Alma, 1854.
Painting by an unknown artist.

The 78th Highlanders (Ross-shire Buffs) at Lucknow, 1857.
Painting by the Chevalier L.W. Desanges.

Signallers of the 72nd (Duke of Albany's Own)
Highlanders, Afghanistan 1879.

Maxim Gun, 2nd battalion
Seaforth Highlanders, Dover 1898.

1st battalion Seaforth Highlanders and 1st battalion
Queen's Own Cameron Highlanders at the Battle of the Atbara, 1898.
Painting by Corporal John Farquharson, Seaforth Highlanders.

1st battalion Queen's Own Cameron Highlanders at the surrender of
General Prinsloo's Boer army, South Africa, 1900.
Painting by W. Skeoch-Cumming.

The 7th (Service) battalion Queen's Own Cameron Highlanders
captures Hill 70, Loos, 1915.
Painting by Joseph Gray.

The pipes and drums of 2nd battalion Seaforth Highlanders, June 1916. Second from the left is Drummer Walter Ritchie, who was to be awarded the Victoria Cross for gallantry at the Battle of the Somme, which began the following week.

Warrant Officers and NCOs of 1st battalion Seaforth Highlanders, Mesopotamia, 1916.

Corporal McGillivray, 1st battalion Queen's Own Cameron Highlanders, France, 1940. Pastel drawing by Eric Kennington.

The recapture of St Valéry by the 51st Highland Division, 1944.
A girl dressed in a skirt made from a Cameron kilt lost in 1940, with two
pipers of the 5th battalion Queen's Own Cameron Highlanders.

Mortar Platoon of 1st battalion Queen's Own Cameron Highlanders,
Suez Canal Zone, 1951.

Queen's Own Highlanders (Seaforth and Camerons).
Painting by Douglas N. Anderson.

The formation of The Highlanders (Seaforth, Gordons and Camerons)
at Edinburgh on 17 September 1994.

on 5 October 1915 its army had been mobilised and it entered the war on the side of the Central Powers. The Allied response was to send two divisions to the port of Salonika (Thessaloniki) under the command of the French general, Maurice Sarrail, a radical socialist and rival of the commander-in-chief, Joffre. At the time German and Austro-Hungarian forces under the command of Field Marshal August von Mackensen had invaded Serbia and entered Belgrade, while Bulgarian forces had pushed into Macedonia, a move which stymied any Allied attempt to relieve pressure on the Serbs. As a result, Sarrail's divisions were pushed back into Salonika, which rapidly became a huge military base – by the end of the year three French and five British divisions, together with a huge amount of stores and ammunition, were encamped in a perimeter which was 200 miles square and defended by miles of barbed wire. For entirely political reasons the British supported the deployment, which the Germans ridiculed as 'the greatest internment camp in the world' and which prevented vital reinforcements and equipment from being deployed on the Western Front. The new French prime minister, Aristide Briand, had made Salonika a plank in his war strategy and the British did not want to provoke a crisis by insisting on withdrawal. There was also a need to maintain pressure on Bulgaria as a means of helping the Russians, who had suffered a heavy defeat at Gorlice-Tarnow in September. Amongst the first formations to arrive on the Salonika front was 2nd Camerons, which was transferred from France in September 1915 and served with 27th Division.

Most of the British effort was confined to the Struma Valley, where the participants found that the style of fighting seemed to come from a different age. On 30 September three Scottish regiments – 1st Royal Scots, 2nd Camerons and 1st Argylls – moved across the Struma to attack Bulgarian positions in the fortified villages of Karajakoi Bala and Karajakoi Zir, with pipers leading them into battle. As a result of the Allied assault the Bulgarians counter-attacked and, as the 2nd battalion's War Diary reveals, the brunt was borne by the Camerons, who were holding the line on the eastern salient:

> The counter-attack did not develop until after dark but owing to our rifle and machine-gun fire did not get any nearer than within 150 yards of our trench, here they tried to dig themselves in and a few crept forward with bombs which they threw into our trench, wounding several men and Captain Stewart. Much shouting was heard from the enemy but owing to the darkness and crops no large body was seen and when it was light next day the enemy appeared to have abandoned the idea of digging in at close quarters and had hurriedly retired, leaving behind them a machine-gun and two carriages and several dead.

Both objectives were captured with the loss of 1,248 casualties and it was the biggest operation undertaken by British forces in Salonika in 1916. However, it was quickly becoming apparent that the main British losses were not battlefield casualties but men who fell victim to malaria – for every casualty from enemy action, ten found themselves in hospital as a result of illness and some units were unable to function. Dysentery and various enteric diseases also caused havoc and put a great strain on the medical services, but malaria was a constant problem mainly because it was endemic in the area and proved difficult to eradicate. Re-infection was also a problem, for although malaria did not kill men in great numbers – fatalities were confined to one per cent of hospital admissions – it did remove soldiers from operational service and in the worst cases incapacitated men had to be evacuated.

CHAPTER SEVEN

The First World War 1916–19

The major British offensive planned for 1916 was an assault on the German lines in the Somme sector. The tactics produced by Haig, now the overall British commander, were deceptively simple. He aimed to attack the German lines using the maximum force at his disposal, to break the defences and then to move forward to take possession of the area to the rear. To do this the British would attack with the Fourth Army numbering 19 divisions which would, in the words of the Tactical Notes produced for the battle, 'push forward at a steady pace in successive lines, each line adding fresh impetus to the preceding line'. Following an enormous week-long bombardment involving the firing of a million shells along a 25-mile front, the Germans were expected to be in no condition to resist and the British infantry would simply brush the opposition aside as it took possession of the German lines. A creeping barrage would keep the surviving Germans cowering in their trenches. Behind the front lines, from Albert to Amiens the British created a huge rear area with new roads, ammunition dumps and encampments in preparation for the push.

The Somme had been a quiet sector for most of the war and

the Germans had used the long periods of relative inaction to good effect by creating a formidable defensive alignment in the firm chalk downlands. Some of the trenches were 30 feet deep and had been constructed to withstand the heaviest bombardments. The lie of the land also favoured the Germans. A first line incorporated several fortified villages such as Thiepval and Fricourt and a second defensive line had been constructed behind the ridges of the higher ground stretching from Pozières to Combles. Protected by barbed wire, these would provide stern defences and the ensuing battle was to be remembered not for the expected breakthrough but as the killing ground of the British Army. No other battlefield of the First World War created more casualties per square yard and the opening day of the battle, 1 July 1916, produced the bloodiest day for the infantry regiments which took part in the initial attack. From the 11 divisions which began the assault, 57,470 men became casualties – 21,392 killed or missing, 35,493 wounded and 585 taken prisoner. It would take another 140 days before the fighting in the sector finally came to an end. The battle was followed in 1917 by equally expensive failures at Arras and Third Ypres or Passchendaele before the Germans launched their spring offensive in 1918, which proved to be their last chance of winning the war.

THE WESTERN FRONT
The Seaforth Highlanders, 2nd, 1/4th, 1/5th, 1/6th, 7th, 8th, 9th battalions

On the opening day of the Battle of the Somme, 1 July 1916, 2nd Seaforth lost 500 casualties during 4th Division's assault on the village of Beaumont Hamel but the battalion had already suffered casualties even before the battle began. Thirteen men had been killed on 25 June by German artillery fire – part of the retaliation during the preliminary British bombardment. The next stage of the battle began on 14 July with the intention of straightening the line before mounting a fresh offensive planned for September. The attacks were centred on the German defensive positions between Guinchy and Martinpuich at Delville Wood, High Wood and Bazentin-le-Petit Wood, names that would always be remembered by the men in the attacking divisions. Amongst them was the 51st (Highland) Division, which went into the attack on High Wood with 5th Division on its right and 19th Division on its left flank. For one officer, recalling the battle in the 51st (Highland) Division's war history, the ground over which the Highland Territorial battalions fought was a scene of devastation which had no equal:

> A giant of steel seemed to have ridden over the proud German defences. Villages were wiped completely out of existence; woods were laid waste. Saddest sight of all, there was not a blade of grass visible. A tumbled heap of rubble marked the spot where the church of Fricourt once stood. Its very gables were powdered to dust. A few gable ends still stood in Mametz. These were gradually being demolished by enemy fire. Trenches were everywhere blown out of recognition.

The damage done to the attacking divisions was equally ruinous. Despite the courage shown by the infantrymen in pressing home the assault on High Wood, wave after wave was beaten off. As their War Diary recorded, one attack by the 1/4th Seaforth on 25 July came to nothing when 'an intense machine-gun fire was opened on the British trenches at the moment when the attackers were mounting the parapet. The troops suffered such losses from this fire that the attack never materialised.' The 51st (Highland) Division suffered 3,500 casualties following two attacks on the heavily defended German position, a situation which its historian recorded as being 'disappointing and dispiriting to all'. As viewed by Lieutenant Ewart Alan Mackintosh, a Gaelic-speaking officer in 1/5th Seaforth, in his poem 'High Wood', the easy enthusiasm of the summer of 1914 had given way to deeper and darker feelings:

> The wild war pipes were calling,
> Our hearts were blithe and free
> When we went up the valley
> To the death we could not see.
> Clear lay the wood before us
> In the clear summer weather,
> But broken, broken, broken
> Are the sons of the heather.

Although Mackintosh's family came from Alness in Easter Ross he was born in Brighton and educated at St Paul's School, London, and Christ Church, Oxford, where he studied Classics. On the outbreak of war he enlisted immediately and was commissioned in 1/5th Seaforth Highlanders. Some of his earlier poems, such as 'Cha till McCruimen: Departure of the 4th Camerons' exulted in the excitement of impending battle with its insistence that the volunteers were marching off to war 'with merry hearts and voices singing' but his exposure to battle soon changed his tune. Mackintosh also wrote a number of deservedly popular songs and parodies such as 'High Wood to Waterlot Farm' and 'The Charge of the Light Brigade brought up to Date' but his reputation rests on the much-anthologised poem 'In Memoriam, Private D. Sutherland', which is a bitter reflection on the anguish felt by soldiers following the deaths of men under their command. The incident which prompted the poem was a raid by 1/5th Seaforth on a German trench on 16 May 1916 which resulted in four deaths, including that of Private David Sutherland, who, to Mackintosh's great grief, had to be left behind during the attack.

Three Seaforth New Army battalions took part in the fighting on the Somme. The 7th battalion was involved in the attack of the 9th (Scottish) Division on the German lines at Longueval and Delville Wood, which began on 14 July and cost the battalion 450 casualties. Serving in the same division as the pioneers was 9th Seaforth, whose men undertook the arduous work of repairing roads and building trenches and strongpoints within the divisional area, usually under heavy enemy fire. In the middle of August, 8th Seaforth was part of the 15th (Scottish) Division's contribution to a general attack on the German lines between Guillemont and Thiepval Ridge. Given the size of the Scottish contribution to the Battle of the Somme it was fitting that the last moves involved a large number of Scottish formations, including the 51st (Highland) Division, which was finally able to put behind it the setbacks encountered at High Wood. Not that the task facing the assaulting forces was any easier: following a dreadful late summer the weather deteriorated again in the autumn, making the ground conditions so bad that, according to one Highland officer, 'tracks and paths became lost in oozing mud of the consistency of porridge'.

Against that background Haig decided to make one last push against Beaucourt and Beaumont Hamel, a first-day objective which had come to be regarded by both sides as being impregnable. The attack was due to begin on 24 October but after many postponements finally commenced on 13 November with the explosion of a mine in front of the German lines and the customary artillery barrage. Under the command of Major-General George 'Uncle' Harper, the 51st (Highland) Division attacked with two brigades and one in reserve, using 'leap-frog' tactics as they advanced towards the German lines of defence. On the right 1/6th Black Watch and 1/7th Gordons quickly reached the German front line and took it without difficulty and although 1/8th Argylls and 1/5th Seaforth were checked on the left they were able to fight their way through to the second line. A diary kept by Captain David Sutherland (no relation to the Sutherland memorialised by Mackintosh) described the role played by 1/5th Seaforth in the closing stages of the battle:

> The 5th Seaforth had the honour of leading the attack, one sector of the village, with their left flank on the Auchonvillers-Beaumont Hamel road; their final objective being a German trench line 200 yards east of the village. The enemy's machine-gun fire and uncut wire in the centre held up the advance for a time, so that the barrage went too far ahead while, owing to the dense fog, direction was lost and the attack split up into small parties. Yet, in spite of these difficulties the first German line was easily carried, except for one or two isolated points where the enemy put up a good fight. Dropping into the trench, sentries were posted at the dug-out doors, while a few bombs were sent down as a gentle reminder of our presence.

Harper's tactics worked in that the division achieved its objectives with only 2,200 casualties, killed, wounded or missing. To the soldiers this was a source of great satisfaction as the failure to take High Wood had gained for them the unattractive nickname of 'Harper's Duds' – a play on their HD divisional badge. All that changed after the assault on Beaumont Hamel. As Harper watched the walking wounded making their way back to the line two days later he overheard one of his Jocks remarking: 'Onyway, they winna ca' us Hairper's Duds noo.'

Early in 1917, the German high command decided to shorten the line between Arras and the Aisne by constructing new and heavily fortified defences which would be their new 'final' position behind the Somme battlefield. Known to the Allies as the

Hindenburg Line this formidable construction shortened the front by some 30 miles and created an obstacle which would not be taken until the end of the war. The withdrawal began on 16 March and as the Germans retired they laid waste to the countryside, leaving a devastated landscape in which the cautiously pursuing Allies had to build fresh trench systems. The new situation led to proposals for a new Allied attack on the shoulders of the Somme salient, with the French attacking in the south at Chemin des Dames while the British and Canadians would mount a supporting offensive at Arras and Vimy Ridge. Prior to the British attack there would be a huge and violent bombardment, with 2,879 guns firing 2,687,000 shells over a five-day period, making it heavier and more lethal than the barrage that had preceded the Somme in the previous summer.

The Battle of Arras involved seven battalions of The Seaforth Highlanders (2nd, 1/4th, 1/5th, 1/6th, 7th, 8th, 9th). They were part of the force of 44 Scottish infantry battalions (out of 124) which took part in the fighting. The battle began in the early morning of 9 April 1917 in a biting wind which sent snow flurries scudding across the countryside, but despite the wintry weather the portents were good. For the first time the assault battalions found that the artillery had done its job by destroying the wire, and new types of gas shells had fallen in the rear areas, killing German transport horses and making the movement of guns impossible. Within a few hours the German line had been penetrated to a depth of two miles and in one of the most astonishing feats of the war the Canadian divisions swept on to take the previously impregnable German positions on the gaunt features of Vimy Ridge. The first day of the assault was a triumph for the British and the Canadians, who succeeded in taking their first objectives and then regrouping to attack the second and third lines of defence. The first phase of the battle encouraged hopes that this might be the long-awaited breakthrough and some units were surprised both by the ease of their attack and the lack of German resistance. For example, all the Seaforth battalions achieved their first-day objectives and the 2nd battalion enjoyed the heady sensation of advancing almost five miles into German-held territory. In other sectors Scottish battalions enjoyed equal levels of success, some moving forward so quickly that they found themselves coming under friendly fire from their own guns. It was at this point that things began to fall apart.

Despite the initial successes the British advance had been irregular and some units were held up by German defensive positions which had escaped the barrage and were still able to inflict heavy casualties on the attacking forces. A huge explosion triggered by the deliberate detonation of a German ammunition dump held up the attack of 1/5th Seaforth but their day ended, as it did for all the attacking battalions, with ground gained and the possibility of taking more. As night fell the weather deteriorated, leaving the infantrymen in forward positions exposed, hungry and bitterly cold, as they had been forbidden to wear or carry their greatcoats during the attack. Battalion war diaries speak of men lying huddled together for warmth, their condition made worse by the failure of supplies to get through to them due to congestion on the roads.

However, Arras did not represent a breakthrough. By the time the fighting ended at the beginning of May any hope of defeating the Germans had disappeared and the losses had multiplied. The British suffered around 159,000 casualties, a daily rate of 4,076 (higher than the Somme's 2,943), and the stuffing had been knocked out of many of the formations which had been involved in a month of hard fighting against a heavily reinforced enemy. The Seaforth casualties were particularly high: the 2nd battalion lost 526 in an attack on Fampoux, including the loss of three company commanders, and the 8th battalion suffered 300 casualties during the attack on Guemappe on 23 April. It was the last time in the war when so many Scottish formations would be on the same battlefield at the same time. Later in the year, at the Third Battle of Ypres, also known as Passchendaele, all three Scottish divisions containing Seaforth battalions – 9th, 15th and 51st – were again involved in the fighting to deepen the British-held Ypres salient. The battle lasted four months and accounted for a quarter of a million casualties, 70,000 of them killed or drowned in the lagoons of mud which covered the battlefield. Now serving in 1st Camerons, John Jackson never forgot the shell holes which littered the battlefield: 'These holes were often ten to twelve feet deep and full up at this time with dirty, slimy water. At the bottom of them in many cases could be seen the bodies of dead men and mules, together with parts of wagons, the whole creating a stench that was rotten and sickening.' The year ended with the Battle of Cambrai, when tanks were first used in large numbers to smash through the German lines. This time the expected breakthrough occurred, with tanks penetrating the German lines to a depth of five miles within the first ten hours, but the action was not exploited and 1917 ended in frustration for the Allies on the Western Front. Cambrai also saw the death of the poet Ewart Alan Mackintosh, who was killed in action on 21 November with 1/4th Seaforth when the 51st (Highland) Division advanced over Flesquières Ridge. The final lines of his last-ever poem, 'War, The Liberator', were a fitting epitaph, not just to him but to all of the Scots who had served as regulars and volunteers between 1915 and 1917 and knew what it was like to face the shock of battle:

> Now in all the time to come, memory will cover us,
> Trenches that we did not lose, charges that we made,
> Since a voice, when first we heard shells go shrilling
>   over us,
> Said within us, 'This is Death – and I am not afraid!'

All the Seaforth battalions on the Western Front were involved in the fighting of 1918 which saw the Germans mount a huge offensive which was beaten back at great cost. When the attack came, as Lieutenant-Colonel W. Petty, 9th Seaforth, recorded, it was as ferocious as anything the Scots had experienced during their three years on the Western Front:

> By the evening of 23rd March, the situation was very critical and patrols sent out by the 9th battalion, now holding the east end of St Pierre Vaast Wood, reported the enemy massing for attack, particularly on the right, where he appeared to be already some way to our rear. Before dawn on 24th March, vast hordes of Germans came on in massed formation, blowing trumpets and whistles and uttering loud hochs and yells. They were mown down time and again, until no more headway could be made for the heaps of dead and wounded, when there ensued a short respite.

By the end of the first day alone the Allies had sustained 38,000 casualties, the majority in the Fifth Army, in which 9th Seaforth was serving, and for a time it seemed that the Germans might indeed break through and turn the Allied line. However, that proved not to be the case. For all the success the Germans enjoyed in the initial assault, they had shot their bolt and by the end of the summer the war was entering its final stages (see below). All the New Army battalions of The Seaforth Highlanders were disbanded in 1919.

Queen's Own Cameron Highlanders, 1st, 5th, 6th, 7th battalions

Following the Battle of Loos the strength of the 1/4th battalion fell to below 500 men and it was gradually broken up during the course of 1916, with men being drafted to reinforce other

battalions. During the early stages of the Battle of the Somme, 5th
Camerons lost 446 casualties while taking part in the 9th (Scottish)
Division's attack on 14 July; the 6th and 7th battalions fought with
15th (Scottish) Division during their assault on the German lines at
Contalmaison the following month. In September Haig decided to
attack the Germans' Third Line of defences in the sector between
Beaucourt and Combles, with the main weight of the assault being
concentrated on the Flers-Courcelette axis (the name by which
the battle is also known). Once again there was a ferocious artillery
bombardment ahead of the main infantry attack, with 828,000
shells being fired over a three-day period. A new weapon, the tank,
was also used in the assault which took place on 15 September.

Compared with earlier attacks on the German defensive
system, the September battle was a success. A large part of the
German line fell into British hands and the tricky objectives of High
Wood and Bazentin Ridge were captured. At one stage during the
fighting at High Wood one company of 1st Camerons suffered so
many casualties that its bayonet strength was reduced to 12 men,
but the Scots' deaths were not in vain. The capture of the position
gave the British a huge advantage by providing better observation
over the German lines and, as Brigadier-General Archibald Home,
a staff officer with the Cavalry Corps, revealed in his diary (held by
the Imperial War Museum), the result was immediately beneficial
for the British:

> Went for a walk to reconnoitre the ground towards Flers
> and walked to the Switch trench between Delville and
> High Wood. It is from here that one can see the value of
> the ridge we have gained and the reason why the Boche
> hung on to it. The ground on the other side lies in front of
> one like an amphitheatre. Le Sars, La Barque, Ligny Thilloy,
> Beaulencourt could all be easily seen and identified. The

ground is open and even in its present state of shell holes could be quickly crossed by cavalry.

During the same phase of the battle 6th Camerons took part in an attack on Martinpuich where it suffered 240 casualties. Two months later, on 5 November, there was a renewed offensive on Butte de Warlencourt, another position which would provide the British with better observation of the German lines. The site of a prehistoric burial ground, it dominated the surrounding countryside but its mass of tunnels and trench systems made it a formidable obstacle. Once again the infantry attack was preceded by an artillery barrage but the wet wintry weather conspired to make life difficult for the British gunners, who were also hampered by shortages of artillery pieces and ammunition. In his diary (held by the Imperial War Museum) Brigadier-General Hugh Tudor, the senior artillery officer in 9th (Scottish) Division, confided that he was by no means certain that the barrage would be of any benefit to the attacking infantry:

> The attack is fixed for tomorrow, in spite of the weather. It seems rather hopeless expecting infantry to attack with any success in this mud. The trench mortars have only their muzzles showing above it. Yesterday we had two barrages by brigades. They seemed fairly good; but I should like more guns. To be effective, a barrage should be an 18-pounder to every 7 yards of enemy front, and the guns should be capable of firing 4 rounds a minute, at least to start with, without the recuperator springs giving out.

Tudor's fears were not misjudged. When the infantry attack began men in 5th Camerons found that they were moving – or more accurately wading and slipping – across ground where the mud was above their knees. Worse, it soon became clear that the divisional artillery had indeed failed to knock out the German positions at Butte de Warlencourt and the attacking infantry battalions came under sustained artillery and machine-gun fire. There were no gains in this action, which symbolised much of the futility which is generally associated with the Battle of the Somme.

The following year saw three battalions in action during the Battle of Arras. During the initial stages of the fighting 6th and 7th Camerons took their first-day objectives and pushed on to take Monchy Le Preux, which had to be held against a fierce German counter-attack, but time was fast running out for the ever more exhausted assault battalions. Increased German resistance and reinforcement meant higher casualties for the attackers. By 23 April the 7th battalion had lost 659 casualties. By then the Germans had reinforced their defensive positions and were able to counter-attack. The result was that the roles were reversed and the British came under a heavy artillery bombardment. The ferocity of the offensive was an unnerving experience and later a Highland Division officer remembered hearing a sergeant encouraging his frightened men with the far from optimistic words: 'Great God A-michty, ye canna a' be killed.' Unfortunately it was not just the German shellfire which caused casualties. On 1 May, during an attack on the chemical factory at Roueux, 5th Camerons was hit by 'friendly fire' – shelling by British artillery due to faulty maps – and lost 300 casualties.

Following the Battle of Arras, the three Cameron New Army battalions were moved north into the Ypres sector and took part in the Third Battle of Ypres, which began on 31 July 1917 and did not come to an end until 6 November, when the village of Passchendaele and the vitally important ridge were captured. Counted as one of the most gruelling battles of the First World War, Third Ypres caused a huge amount of death and misery and the Cameron losses were as heavy as those in any of the battalions which went into the attack along the Ypres salient in the late summer and autumn of 1917: the 5th battalion lost 200 casualties, the 6th battalion lost 296 casualties, including the commanding officer, Colonel J.C. Russell, and the 7th battalion lost 292 casualties. All the gains made during the four-month battle were lost when the Germans mounted their 'Michael' offensive in March, their last opportunity to win the war on the Western Front.

The storm broke in the early hours of the morning of 21 March 1918, when the German artillery produced a huge bombardment which lasted five hours and left the defenders badly shaken and disorientated. Gas and smoke shells added to the confusion, which was increased by an early morning mist, leaving commanders with no exact idea of where and when the infantry attack was coming. In their defensive positions in the Cambrai sector near Beaumetz the 51st (Highland) Division had its first inkling that something was afoot when scouting parties observed thousands of German infantrymen entering the front-line trenches carrying weapons but leaving behind their heavy packs, clearly preparing for an assault.

During the German assault 1st Camerons was involved in 1st Division's battle to hold the line at Givenchy, while the three New Army battalions were on the Somme and Arras sectors. So high were the casualties in the 15th (Scottish) Division that it was forced to reduce its brigade strength from four to three battalions. As a result the 6th and 7th battalions were amalgamated to become 6/7th Camerons. Even experienced divisions found themselves in difficulties: as the 9th (Scottish) Division withdrew from its position in front of Gouzeaucourt it lost touch with the neighbouring 47th Division, allowing the left flank to be exposed. The casualties were not just the rank and file – the 51st (Highland) Division lost three out of ten battalion commanders – and over 20,000 soldiers went into captivity. However, despite the heavy losses the Germans had shot their bolt and while they managed to capture a huge salient they had also suffered huge losses – as many as 250,000 men – and by the end of April the Germans' spring offensive was finished. Following its failure the Germans turned their attention to the French armies along the Aisne. Once again the German assault forces achieved an initial success by breaching the opposition's defences, and by 30 May they had reached the Marne, creating a salient 20 miles deep and 30 miles wide. Vigorous counter-attacks frustrated the German advance and British forces were also involved when the newly formed XXII Corps under Lieutenant-General Sir Alexander Godley was deployed in support of the French army in Champagne. Amongst its four divisions were 15th (Scottish) and 51st (Highland), and both of them took part in what became known as the Second Battle of the Marne, which finally halted the German advance in the middle of July. Amongst the battalions which took part in the fighting was 6/7th Camerons.

The battle represented the last best chance for the Germans to win the war, for although they had won large tracts of enemy ground, all the salients had vulnerable flanks which were prone to counter-attack. The Germans had also taken huge casualties, and for the survivors it was dispiriting to see that so little had been gained for so much effort. At the same time, they were aware that the Americans were arriving in France at the rate of 300,000 a month and would soon produce a formidable opposition, with fresh troops and a seemingly limitless supply of weapons and equipment. The beginning of the end came on 8 August, when Australian and Canadian forces attacked the German positions to the east of Amiens with a British and a French corps guarding the flank to the north and south. The attack achieved complete surprise and the Allies were able to advance eight miles in one day, taking over 12,000 German prisoners in the process.

The war now entered its final phase, the so-called 'last

hundred days', which saw the long-awaited breakthrough on the Western Front. One of the last actions involved the 1st Camerons when the British 1st Division attacked the heavily fortified village of Droninghem during the Battle of the Sambre on 7 November. Using improvised rafts it crossed the Sambre Canal under heavy German fire and although it captured the stronghold and forced the Germans to surrender, the battalion lost around 500 casualties. For John Jackson, who had joined up in 1914 and had survived the fighting, that evening's muster was one of his saddest moments: 'When the roll was called our casualties were found to be enormous, and many old friends were no more. It was indeed hard that many of these battle-scarred warriors, having come through the entire war should in this, our last great battle, have their names included in the honoured lists of those "Killed in action".' The 6/7th battalion ended its war on the Loos sector and was disbanded on 25 June 1919.

MESOPOTAMIA AND PALESTINE
The Seaforth Highlanders, 1st battalion

Following the fall of Kut-al-Amara, both 2nd Black Watch and 1st Seaforth, now under the command of Lieutenant-Colonel P.G. Anstruther, were brought up to strength with drafts from home and along with 1st Highland Light Infantry the battalion took part in the renewed offensive which began on 12 December 1916. Two months later Kut was recaptured and General Maude pushed on to Baghdad, continuing his campaign in the furnace-like heat of summer, with the temperature reaching 120 degrees in the shade. During the advance on Baghdad Captain L.A. Lynden Bell kept a diary which gives a good idea of the conditions facing the men in the 1st battalion as they made their way along the Tigris towards the fabled city 'whose blue domes and minarets looked magnificent from the desert'. During the march the weather conditions ranged from heavy rain and high winds through freezing nights to the kind of conditions most soldiers expected in the Middle East:

> Dawn on 9th March revealed a new world around us. We
> marched past crops of potatoes and even broad beans, things
> which seemed to belong to the distant ages. Not far away
> were groups of palm trees, which spoke of the proximity of
> a large town. We continued marching till the sun was high in
> the heavens, and we were once more lost in the desert, out of
> sight of all cultivation. During a halt for breakfast, we heard
> the familiar and unpleasant noise of the enemy's outposts
> being driven in. We moved on again in the afternoon, but
> without becoming engaged with the enemy. At nightfall
> we formed a perimeter camp with the Artillery.

Baghdad eventually fell two days later without much Turkish
opposition. Maude's success was helped by the fact that the Turks
had been forced to withdraw forces to serve on a new front which
had opened in Palestine but he deserves full credit for restoring the
badly battered British and Indian divisions and for taking the war
back to the Turks. Over 9,000 prisoners were taken and the fall of
the city was the first solid Allied triumph of the war. Unfortunately,
Maude died of cholera in November but by then he had created
plans for his forces to advance up the Tigris towards Mosul, with
its vital oilfields, and further up the Euphrates towards Ramadi,
while another force proceeded up the Diyala towards Kirkuk.
During this last phase of the operation 1st Seaforth fought actions at
Moushahdieh, Beled and Istabulat before embarking for Egypt on
New Year's Day, 1918. Following a period of resting and refitting
at Ismailia, 1st Seaforth joined XXI Corps for the final stages of
General Allenby's campaign in Palestine. Its last battle of the war
was fought during the advance to Beit Lid on 20 September, a
tough operation which involved a forced march of 34 miles in

48 hours. At the conclusion of hostilities the battalion was based in Beirut where it remained until March 1919.

SALONIKA
The Seaforth Highlanders, 1st Garrison Battalion
Queen's Own Cameron Highlanders, 2nd, 10th battalions

During the summer of 1916 the British garrison in Salonika received reinforcements, amongst them being 1st Garrison Battalion Seaforth Highlanders which had been raised at Tillicoultry as a second-line force composed mainly of men who were below physical standard, or had been wounded or were over-age. Even so, they found themselves involved in hostile operations on the Struma Front 'contrary to the letter of their enrolment, but not the spirit of the Men'. The main action in Salonika took place in May 1917 with an operation by the French and Serb forces to break through the Bulgarian defensive lines. The British objectives, undertaken by XII Corps, were the heavily defended positions to the west of Lake Doiran but the Allied offensive failed and had to be abandoned on 23 May with the loss of 5,024 British casualties. As happened on the Western Front, the Allied artillery failed to cut the wire and the attacking infantry soon found themselves pinned down by accurate Bulgarian artillery and machine-gun fire. The mountainous terrain also helped the defenders and the commander-in-chief of British Salonika Forces, Lieutenant-General G.F. Milne, was forced to concede that 'our men are not a match for the Bulgar in hill-fighting, though superior on the flat'. (Other problems came from manpower shortages, lack of reliable equipment, especially heavy artillery, and the absence of coherent plans.) For the rest of the year the front remained surprisingly quiet while XVI Corps' activities in the Struma Valley were confined to minor though testing operations such as a successful night attack on a Bulgarian position at Homondos on 14 October 1917, which involved 2nd Camerons. As remembered by Lieutenant (later Major-General) A.L. Collier in an interview held by the Imperial War Museum, the attack took the battalion across hard ground consisting of sunken tracks and dried-up river beds:

> The whole area was a maze of dilapidated trenches and straggling barbed-wire entanglements, partially concealed by thick vegetation. Coarse grass from three to six feet high grew in patches, and this grass, in addition to concealing obstacles, made silent movement at night almost impossible for a body of troops of any size. The vegetation was not, however, sufficient to conceal the movement of a large force by daylight, as the whole plain was completely overlooked by the Bulgar position in the foothills to the north.

During the winter Greece finally entered the war on the Allied side, following the abdication of the pro-German King Constantine, and at last the Allies were rewarded for their long-standing military presence in Salonika. At the same time Sarrail was sacked and replaced first by General M.L.A. Guillaumat and then by General Louis Franchet D'Espérey, who brought the campaign to a conclusion in the summer of 1918. Weakened by German troop withdrawals the Bulgarian army failed to halt the last assault of the war, which began on 15 September and ended a fortnight later when the Bulgarian front was split. On 29 September French forces entered Skopje and the following day Bulgaria requested an armistice. D'Espérey was keen to continue his advance up through the Balkans to threaten Germany's southern flank, and his troops were already crossing the Danube when the war came to an end on 11 November. At the same time, Milne moved his British forces up to the Turkish frontier but his hopes of attacking Turkey ended when the Turks signed an armistice on 31 October. Elements of British forces remained in the area into 1919, serving as peacekeepers, and for most of them it was a dispiriting end to a campaign which had tied up huge numbers of men and materiel for no obvious strategic gains. Although the British Salonika Force listed a modest 18,000 casualties from combat, this was overshadowed by the 481,000 who had succumbed to illness, mainly malaria.

Following the armistice, 2nd Camerons was moved by ship as part of 27th Division's intervention to expel German forces from Georgia and did not return to Britain until May 1919. There was also a move for the Seaforth's 1st Garrison Battalion, which ended the war garrisoning Constanza and various towns in the Dobrudja province of Romania and was not disbanded until June 1919. For the 10th (Lovat Scouts) Camerons the war ended in France after the battalion was moved to the Western Front during the summer of 1918.

CHAPTER EIGHT

The Second World War 1939–42

Following the conclusion of hostilities there was an immediate and dramatic reduction in the size of the peacetime army. All New Army battalions were disbanded and there were painful reductions in the size of the Territorial Army, which affected both The Seaforth Highlanders and Queen's Own Cameron Highlanders. In 1922 The Seaforth Highlanders' 4th and 5th battalions were amalgamated as 4/5th Seaforth Highlanders, an arrangement which lasted from 1921 until 1938 when the expansion of the Territorial Army restored the old order by recreating the 4th and 5th battalions to meet the threat posed by Nazi Germany. At the same time 4th Camerons was reconstituted as the regiment's Territorial battalion while the 5th battalion was restored in 1939. Recognition was also given to the unofficial affiliation which had existed between Queen's Own Cameron Highlanders and the 10th (Scottish) Battalion, The King's Liverpool Regiment, which had come into being as part of the creation of the Territorial Force in 1908. During the war the relationship had flourished and two battalions of the Liverpool Scottish (as they were also known) served on the Western Front. The medical officer of the 1st Liverpool Scottish, Captain N.G.

Chavasse, had the distinction of winning the Victoria Cross in August 1916 and a posthumous bar in July 1917. In September 1937 the Liverpool Scottish was redesignated as 1st Liverpool Scottish, Queen's Own Cameron Highlanders. A 2nd battalion was added in 1939.

For the regular battalions of both regiments the post-war years brought different fortunes. The 1st Seaforth returned to Scotland in 1919 and was based at Glencorse and Fort George, with a deployment in Bridge of Allan and Cowdenbeath during the coal miners' strike in 1921. This was followed by a five-year tour of duty in aid of the civil power in Dublin and Belfast. From 1926 to 1933 the battalion spent time at Aldershot and Dover before being deployed in Palestine and Egypt during a difficult period known as the Arab Revolt. Palestine had become a British mandated territory under the League of Nations, a form of trust by which the country was administered under the supervision of a Permanent Mandates Commission. Under its terms Britain had also included the Balfour Declaration of 1917, a wartime pledge of support for the creation of a Jewish homeland in Palestine which attracted 56,000 Jewish settlers. As the region already contained 600,000 Arabs the post-war immigration had the potential to cause trouble but during the war Britain was anxious to receive, and to continue receiving, Jewish money and support for the war effort.

In 1922, aware of mounting Arab resistance to the declaration and the growing importance of the region's oil supplies, Britain distanced itself from its wartime policy by laying down economic guidelines for immigration and excluding neighbouring Transjordan, an important ally, from the areas available for resettlement. As tensions mounted between the rival populations in the 1930s the British produced two partition plans aimed at providing a workable settlement for the Jewish and Arab populations. Neither succeeded in achieving its objectives and that failure left the British Army holding the line as fighting broke out between the two communities in 1936. As Colonel John Sym's history makes clear it was 'a very trying period for, although the daily routine involved all the activities of a frontier operation, escorts to convoys, ambush parties, patrols and picqueting, it was not until the bullet struck, or the bomb burst that one could differentiate between friend and foe'. At the beginning of 1937 the battalion moved to Hong Kong before being posted to Shanghai in China as part of the British garrison which was based there during a protracted stand-off between China and Japan.

During the same period 2nd Seaforth was in India from 1919 to 1932, when it moved to Palestine before returning to Scotland in 1934. During the stay in India the battalion was based variously at Meerut, Landi Kotal, Nowshera, Lahore, Jhansi and Rawalpindi. From an operational point of view the high point was a deployment under the command of Lieutenant-Colonel K.A.N. Anderson to the North-West Frontier Province in the summer of 1930 to crush an uprising of dissident Afridi tribesmen known as Red Shirts. To counter the threat two brigade groups were sent into the area to secure the Khajuri Plain to the south of the Khyber Pass; by constructing strongpoints and improving lines of communication they were able to deny the use of the area to the insurgents and to protect the routes into Peshawar.

The Camerons also spent a good part of the inter-war years in India. The 1st battalion was based there from 1919 to 1925, when it was deployed on internal security duties in the Kurram Valley in the North-West Frontier Province and also spent time in Calcutta and Rawalpindi. For the next five years the battalion moved to Burma and returned to India in 1930. This was followed by a move to Sudan in 1930 before 1st Camerons returned to Britain in 1936, to be based at Catterick in Yorkshire. As the home service battalion 2nd

Camerons spent two years in Ireland (1920–22) and three years with the army of occupation in Germany (1923–26) before returning to Edinburgh. On 14 July 1927 the battalion provided the Guard of Honour at the opening of the Scottish National War Memorial in Edinburgh Castle, which commemorates the Scottish dead of the First World War. Following five years in Aldershot the battalion moved to Palestine, where it was involved in internal security duties, and moved to Ahmednagar in India in November 1938.

All the while, the international situation was deteriorating and by the end of the 1930s war with Adolf Hitler's Nazi Germany was inevitable. In 1938 Prime Minister Neville Chamberlain seemed to have bought 'peace in our time' following his negotiations with Hitler in Munich which gave the Germans a free hand in the Sudetenland and subsequently in Bohemia and Moravia. It proved to be the calm before the storm. Having signed a peace pact with the Soviet Union, Hitler then felt free to invade Poland at the beginning of September. Chamberlain, who would be replaced as prime minister by Winston Churchill the following year, had no option but to declare war – Britain and Poland were bound by treaty – but the country's armed forces were hardly in a fit condition to fight a modern war. The British Army could put together only four divisions as an expeditionary force for Europe, six infantry and one armoured division in the Middle East, a field division and a brigade in India, two brigades in Malaya and a modest scattering of imperial garrisons elsewhere. Years of neglect and tolerance of old-fashioned equipment meant that the army was ill-prepared to meet the modern German forces in battle and British industry was not geared up to make good those deficiencies. Once again in the nation's history it seemed that Britain was going to war with the equipment and mentality of previous conflicts. Events in Poland quickly showed that Germany was a ruthless and powerful enemy: the country fell within 18 days of the invasion, allowing Hitler to turn his attention to defeating France. To bolster the French the British government deployed a British Expeditionary Force (BEF) which included Regular and Territorial battalions of The Seaforth Highlanders and Queen's Own Cameron Highlanders.

FRANCE AND FLANDERS
The Seaforth Highlanders, 2nd(old), 4th, 5th, 6th battalions
Queen's Own Cameron Highlanders, 1st, 4th battalions

For 2nd Seaforth the Second World War had opened with the return of reservists – the battalion was stationed at Maryhill Barracks in Glasgow – and this was followed by the immediate deployment to France with 17th Infantry Brigade, 5th Division, as part of the BEF. This took them to the Maginot Line, which ran from the French–Belgian border south towards Switzerland and was France's main defensive position in the east. In January 1940 the 51st (Highland) Division landed in France under the command of Major-General Victor Fortune. As it was composed entirely of Territorial infantry battalions the decision was taken to reinforce it with three regular battalions, one for each brigade. One of these was 2nd Seaforth, which joined 4th Seaforth and 4th Camerons in 152 Brigade; in return 6th Seaforth moved out of the division and took the 2nd battalion's place in 17th Brigade, 5th Division. At the same time 1st Camerons crossed over to France under the command of Lieutenant-Colonel Douglas Wimberley, who had fought a spirited battle with the War Office to allow the Cameron Highlanders to continue wearing the kilt. Unlike his famous predecessor, Sir Alan Cameron of Erracht, who had refused to wear the 'befringed frippery of English pantaloons' (see Chapter One), Wimberley had to bow to the official diktat, but while the regiment's battalions wore standard khaki battle-dress they also managed to retain the use of the kilt for special occasions. While in France 1st Camerons was inspected by the regiment's colonel-in-chief, King George VI, on 5 December 1939 and the battalion War Diary recorded a historic moment which is also commemorated by a regimental pipe tune 'The Royal Blue Hackle', a slow march composed by Lance-Corporal J. Margach:

> Lt-Colonel Wimberley asked our Colonel-in-Chief if the Battalion, as a mark of distinction, might wear a hackle in their balmorals as had long been done on the topee, in India, with Service dress. His Majesty was pleased to agree with this request and that the hackle should be of Royal Blue, and not White, to mark the fact that the Camerons were a Royal regiment, the only other Royal Highland regiment being the Black Watch, who wore the Red Hackle.

This period was known as the 'phoney war', with both sides adopting a live-and-let-live philosophy, but all that came to an end on 10 May when German land and air forces attacked across the Low Countries as a prelude to invading France. Taken aback by the ferocity and speed of the German advance into Belgium, the BEF began its long retreat back to the Channel ports and the eventual evacuation from the beaches at Dunkirk. For 1st Camerons this meant engaging the enemy along the River Escaut; one incident recorded in the diary of Lieutenant-Colonel G.P. Miller and published in the regimental records is worthy of note:

> During the day [18 May at Lessines], while we were preparing the bridge and crossings for demolition, refugees were pouring through us. The Belgian mayor came to me and stated that there were about two hundred wounded men in a convent, with only one girl to look after them. Could I supply transport to evacuate these wounded? My reply was that I was afraid I had not sufficient transport,

but I would try to make them comfortable. During this conversation a man arrived at my headquarters informing me that there were some nuns amongst the refugees, who would be only too willing to nurse the wounded. Later that night, when we withdrew, we were fired upon from the windows of the convent.

While the BEF was involved in the great escape at Dunkirk the 51st (Highland) Division was deployed along a defensive line to the south-west of Abbeville near the mouth of the River Somme. Sixty miles away to the south-west lay the small port of St Valéry-en-Caux with the road via Dieppe forming a southern boundary. The division had started the war under French command in the Saar region where their armoured support was provided by the Mark VIb light tanks of the Lothians and Borders Horse, a yeomanry regiment, but following the initial German onslaught they had been compelled to withdraw towards the fortified positions in the French Maginot Line. The speed of the German army's armoured assault meant that the division was cut off from the rest of the BEF and its fortunes were now tied firmly to the French Third Army under the command of General Besson. During this difficult period it became clear to the British high command that some elements in the French army were considering suing for peace. As these included the commander-in-chief, General Maxime Weygand, and Marshal Philippe Pétain, the renowned commander of the First World War, the threat had to be taken seriously. Churchill was determined to keep France in the war at all costs and that necessity was to play a part in determining the fate of the Highland Division. If the French were to sue for an armistice, as had been threatened, it would allow their powerful navy to fall into German hands and make an invasion of Britain more likely. At the same time, Churchill wanted to withdraw the bulk of the BEF through Dunkirk, even though that decision gave the impression to the French that their allies were pulling out and leaving them to their fate. As the 51st (Highland) Division continued to pull further back into Flanders the political thinking in London was to have a decisive effect on what happened to them in the days ahead. Basically, Churchill's policy was to keep the 51st (Highland) Division in France as a means of maintaining pressure on the French to stay in the war.

On 4 June the division supported a French attack made by the remnants of the French armoured and artillery forces along the Mareuil Ridge, to the south of Abbeville, but although the French fought with great determination they were outnumbered and outgunned. This was the last full-scale Allied attack of 1940 in France but even as it took place the last of the BEF was being picked up from the Dunkirk beaches. Whatever the outcome of the attack on the Mareuil Ridge the 51st (Highland) Division was now on its own, together with the remnants of the 1st Armoured Division. The following day the Germans launched a fresh offensive along the line between the Somme and the Aisne and the overwhelming power of their offensive sealed the division's fate as it withdrew to the coast. It was a time of desperate fighting and confusion when men were exhausted both by the need to retreat and to fight a rampant enemy. As the 4th Seaforth War Diary recorded on 10 June it was also a time of great confusion, when anything could have happened:

> In the town [Martigny] traffic and refugees were causing confusion in the dark. It was proving impossible to prevent unauthorised persons from crossing the road bridge. Drivers were being directed loudly, by 154 Brigade traffic control, to 'Drive to Frecamp', to the detriment of security. A strange officer, in a Vauxhall car, claiming to be a Staff Officer of B Brigade, attempted to interrogate the Officer

in charge of the road bridge, but disappeared before he could be apprehended.

To the end, Fortune hoped to pull his division out of Le Havre but after almost two weeks of hard fighting, on 12 June he was forced to surrender to his opponents, the German 7th Panzer Division led by General Erwin Rommel. More than 10,000 British troops went into captivity at St Valéry-en-Caux and, as the historian Saul David has pointed out in his history of the campaign, there is little doubt that they 'paid a heavy price for the miscalculations of the Government'. For The Seaforth Highlanders the surrender meant the loss of its 2nd and 4th battalions, and the Camerons lost their 4th battalion, but every Highland regiment was also affected and in the Highland areas of Scotland there were scarcely any families who were left untouched by the loss of the division. For those captured the war meant five long years in camps in Germany and Poland where the men were given agricultural work or laboured in coal mines, a dispiriting fate for any soldier.

ERITREA AND NORTH AFRICA
The Seaforth Highlanders, 2nd (new), 5th battalions
Queen's Own Cameron Highlanders, 2nd, 5th battalions

Orders for mobilisation reached 2nd Camerons while the battalion cricket team was engaged in a match against the Small Arms School at Ahmednagar in the last week of July. Within days the battalion had left for Bombay, where they embarked 'under sealed orders' on SS *Karanja*. Their destination was Egypt, where they were brigaded with 4/7th Rajputs and 1/6th Rajputana Rifles in 11th Indian Infantry Brigade as part of the forces for the defence of Egypt against the threat of Italian attack. This was the Western Desert Force, which consisted of 4th Indian Division and 7th Armoured Division, and was commanded by Major-General Richard O'Connor. In the uneasy period before Italy entered the war on 11 June 1940 the Allied forces in Egypt spent the time training for the expected onslaught from Libya, where the Italians had deployed 250,000 troops. It was an anxious period, as Italy was in a position to threaten Britain's control of the Mediterranean and its vital lines of communication with India and the Far East. As the 4th Indian Division's history makes clear, it was time well spent:

> The hours of work were long, from sunrise to sunset; after dark no lights were allowed, but as the nights were short, this was not much of a handicap at this time of the year. The British troops were so tanned from the blazing sun, from which there was no shade, that they became as dark as the Indians, while the way in which all fraternised made this encampment in the desert a friendly and happy one.

The Italian attack began in the middle of September and they moved quickly into Egyptian territory capturing Sidi Barrani to threaten a major invasion of Egyptian territory. In response the British decided to counter-attack before the Italian advance gathered any momentum and 2nd Camerons was involved in the first part of the offensive, on 22 October against Italian positions at Maktila. The battalion also played a role in the attack on Nibeiwa Camp, which resulted in the capture of 2,000 Italians and was the prelude to the retaking of Sidi Barrani on 10 December. Taken by surprise by the determination and ferocity of the British offensive, the Italians quickly capitulated to O'Connor's much smaller force of 30,000 soldiers. As a result of this first Allied victory of the war, 38,000 Italians, 237 artillery pieces and 73 tanks fell into British hands, and the only remaining sign of the Italian presence was at Sollum, Fort Capuzzo and Sidi Omar. As a result of the easy victory and the lack of any Italian response General Sir Archibald Wavell, GOC Middle East, decided to move the 4th (Indian) Division from Egypt to East Africa where the Italian commander, the Duke of Aosta, had opened his campaign by invading Sudan. Another formation, 5th (Indian) Division, was also sent to reinforce the local garrison, which consisted of the Sudan Defence Force and three British infantry battalions. In the face of these aggressive Allied measures the Duke of Aosta started withdrawing his forces back into Ethiopia through Eritrea, a land of desert plains and high rocky mountains. The main battle of the campaign was fought at Keren where the Italians occupied positions on high ground overlooking the main road through the Ascidira Valley. It was an imposing obstacle of razor-like ridges and peaks which rose to over 6,000 feet, and the initial attacks at the beginning of February failed to make any impression on the Italian defences.

Despite the difficulties, on the first day of the battle, 3 February, 2nd Camerons succeeded in taking their objective, which was subsequently renamed Cameron Ridge and was used as a jumping-off point for further attacks. The fighting resumed on 15 March with the overall commander, General Sir William Platt, issuing a stark warning to his men: 'It is going to be a bloody battle against both enemy and ground. It will be won by the side that lasts the longest.' Twelve days later the issue was decided by the grit and determination of the two Indian divisions. Some of the hardest fighting involved 2nd Camerons during the attacks on the enemy positions on Mount Sanchil and Brig's Peak. The battalion War Diary provides a good idea of the conditions facing the men when they went into the attack:

> Zero-hour arrived and the artillery opened. B and C Companies advanced over the brow of the hill, with D Company following C. A Company, for the moment, was kept back.

The enemy put down a hail of mortar and machine-gun defensive fire, but it was quite impossible to see the result on either side owing to dust and smoke, though it was afterwards learnt that a large number of our casualties were sustained during the first two hundred yards of this advance.

The victory at Keren persuaded the Italians to withdraw from Asmara and the capture of the port of Massawa on 8 April signalled the end of Italian resistance in Eritrea, but it came at a price. The British suffered 3,767 casualties killed or wounded and amongst that number were 209 men of 2nd Camerons.

As a result of the successful outcome of the campaign Wavell was able to return 4th Indian Division to North Africa, where Egypt was under a new threat following the arrival of German forces, the Afrika Korps, under the command of General Erwin Rommel. A series of successful assaults had retaken all the ground won by the Allies in the previous year and Cyrenaica was in danger of falling into Rommel's hands. By the beginning of April the vital port of Tobruk was under threat and Churchill ordered that it had to be held at all costs. His directive also ordered the Western Desert Force to counter-attack and engage all enemy forces between Tripoli and El Agheila, and in so doing to regain ascendancy in Libya. It was easier said than done. Rommel renewed his attack at the beginning of May and as the Allies withdrew, Tobruk was left isolated. Despite offering stout resistance the garrison was forced to surrender on 21 June. Amongst them was 2nd Camerons, which continued fighting for a further day before its commanding officer, Lieutenant-Colonel C.S. Duncan, ordered all able-bodied men to break out and attempt to reach safety in Egypt. For the rest it was a bitter moment, but Duncan insisted that he and his men should be allowed to march into captivity with pipes playing and all the honours of war. Later in the year, on 20 December, a new 2nd battalion came into being by redesignating the regiment's 4th battalion. The original Territorial battalion had been lost at St Valéry but was immediately reconstituted in Inverness and was deployed in Aruba in the Dutch West Indies between August 1940 and February 1942.

The 51st (Highland) Division had also been resurrected, in its case with the help of another equally distinguished Scottish formation, the 9th (Scottish) Division, which had come into being during the First World War as part of Kitchener's New Army. It was renumbered as the 51st and given the famous HD divisional sign, and quickly started building up its own esprit de corps with the divisional headquarters in Rothes, Banffshire, under the command of Major-General Neil Ritchie. Serving in the reconstituted division were a new 2nd Seaforth battalion raised by Lieutenant-Colonel George Murray and 5th Seaforth, which both served in 152 Brigade with 5th Camerons. At the end of March 1942 the division, now under the command of Major-General Douglas Wimberley, moved to Aldershot, where they came under the command of General Bernard Montgomery, GOC South-East Command, a soldier with whom they would be closely associated for the rest of the war. Later that summer the entire division set sail for North Africa, a long and bruising voyage round the Cape of Good Hope which lasted 59 days, and for most of the men felt even longer.

Once in Egypt the division started training for desert warfare, getting used to the heat and hardening itself for the shock of battle. This was a difficult period for the British forces in the country. Cairo was under threat and it seemed inevitable that another enemy assault would lead to the collapse of British power in North Africa. Morale was low and defeat seemed inevitable. At that point Churchill decided to change the command structure by appointing Montgomery to take over the Eighth Army. It proved to be an inspired choice and the new commander showed a sure touch in directing his first battle – the Battle of Alamein, which began on 23 October and turned out to be the first decisive British land victory of the war. To the operation Montgomery brought scrupulous planning and instilled a belief in the Eighth Army that they had the training and the equipment to defeat an enemy which was not unbeatable. It was also a set-piece battle similar to the kind that had been fought in the latter stages of the First World War, with soldiers advancing under a heavy barrage and battalions leap-frogging forward to take their objectives.

The attacking force moved off shortly after 10 p.m., each battalion being guided by a navigation officer watching his compass and counting his paces to ensure accuracy. All the first objectives were quickly taken with the follow-up forces passing through the first wave. By dawn the following day the second objectives had been taken and the battle moved into its next phase, which Montgomery had promised would be a 'dog-fight'. All the time shelling continued on either side and tank battles raged as British Sherman tanks engaged the enemy lines. In some parts of the line the fighting was more fierce than others but as Alastair Borthwick, 5th Seaforth, recorded in his autobiography, the experience of battle almost defied description:

> The noise is unbelievable. If one shell be fired from one 25-pounder gun at night, the Infantryman first sees a flash far behind him and a few seconds later hears the sound of the gun. Again there is a slight pause; and far overhead a shrill sound, somewhere between a whine and a sigh and small wind blowing across the strings of a harp, grows in volume and deepens in tone until the shell roars into the ground ahead of him. There is a red flash, and an explosion which has a distinct metallic clang in it.

This was the common lot of every soldier who fought at Alamein – of being under constant mortar and shellfire and of being pinned down by artillery as the forward formations attempted to make the final breakthrough. However, it could not last, as the speed and aggression of the Allied assault had broken the enemy's will to resist. On 3 November Operation Supercharge was put into effect as British, Indian and New Zealand forces fought their way out of the German lines of barbed wire and minefields to allow the armoured forces to begin the chase after the now-retreating German and Italian forces. Soon Montgomery's advancing men were passing well-known names which had become familiar to the Allies during the years of attack and retreat – Benghazi, Sidi Barrani, El Agheila, El Adem, Mersa Brega – as they raced towards the strategically important goal of the port of Tripoli. Ahead lay Tunis, the next objective, and ahead too was the battle for the Mareth Line, where the 51st (Highland) Division found itself in some of the fiercest fighting of that phase of the advance. All three Seaforth and Cameron battalions were involved in the subsequent Battle of Wadi Akarit on 6 April, when they took part in an impressive brigade attack against heavily defended German positions on the Djebel Roumana Ridge. The fighting lasted all day and at nightfall the Germans began pulling back, leaving the road open to the 51st (Highland) Division. Wadi Akarit was the last encounter with the Germans in North Africa; from Tunisia in the west the First Army was approaching to rendezvous with the Eighth Army and the fall of Tunis on 7 May signalled the end of the fighting in North Africa.

MADAGASCAR
The Seaforth Highlanders, 6th battalion

Having taken part in the retreat to Dunkirk and the subsequent evacuation to Britain, 6th Seaforth played a role in one of the lesser-known campaigns of the war when it was part of a force raised at the beginning of 1942 to capture the French colony of Madagascar off the east African coast. Initially, the governor of the island had thrown in his lot with the Free French forces under the command of General Charles de Gaulle, but he changed his mind and resigned his post after the destruction of the French fleet by the Royal Navy at Mers-el-Kebir (an operation ordered by Churchill to prevent the French warships being used by the Germans). He was replaced by a representative of the Vichy government, General Armand Leon Annet. That altered the strategic balance in the region as the Vichy government collaborated with the Germans, and in March 1942 the British received intelligence that Germany had persuaded Japan to occupy the island as a means of gaining naval superiority in the Indian Ocean, a move that would threaten strategic supply routes. To prevent that happening a British invasion force, Force 121, was put together under the command of Major-General Robert Sturges, consisting of 17th and 29th Brigades (with 13th Brigade as a strategic reserve) and No. 5 Commando. In the first major amphibious operation of the conflict and the first ambitious landings since Gallipoli in 1915, Sturges's primary task was to capture the northern naval base at Diégo Suarez with support from a naval task force under the command of Rear-Admiral Neville Syfret.

With air cover provided by aircraft of the Fleet Air Arm flying from the carriers *Indomitable* and *Illustrious*, the first assault was made against Diégo Suarez on 5 May. Although Operation Ironclad achieved complete surprise the resistance was surprisingly strong and the fighting for the port and the town of Antsirane (now Antseranana) lasted for three days before the French capitulated. Before their night attack on 6 May, 6th Seaforth marched 20 miles along 'an abominably dusty track' and went into the attack on the left with 2nd Royal Scots Fusiliers in the centre and 2nd Northamptons on the right. Much of the fighting ended up being close-quarter combat involving generous use of the bayonet. In his history of the 6th battalion Jim Stockman provided a graphic account of the moment when bayonet practice was translated into the reality of battle:

> As I kept going, I suddenly came across this huge Senegalese coming at me. For a moment I panicked, hesitated. Then, on thankful impulse, stopped him in his tracks by thrusting forward and shoving the bayonet right through him until it emerged on the other side.
>
> At first, I did not realise the ferocity with which I had struck him and then found to my horror that I could not pull it out again. I had to fire a round, twist savagely and pull in order to disengage it from his body.

The Seaforth charge succeeded in taking the Vichy French position and Antsirane fell overnight. It was not the end of the struggle as the French governor retreated to the south of the island with the rump of his forces. In the original plans for Ironclad the capture of the naval port had been deemed to be sufficient, but following its capture the South African prime minister, General Jan Smuts, insisted that the whole island and its 900 miles of coastline should be captured. During a lull in operations 6th Seaforth was moved to India on 11 June, when 17th Brigade deployed to the subcontinent to join the rest of 5th Division for the defence of India following the Japanese invasion of Burma. The campaign reopened ahead of the rainy season on 10 September when 29th Brigade and the East African forces landed at the ports of Majunga in the north-west and Morondava on the west of the island. Although progress was slow, the capital, Tananarive, fell two weeks later and the last major action was at Andriamanalina on 18 October. Annet surrendered near Ilhosy, in the south of the island, on 5 November. During the operations in Madagascar, 6ᵗʰ Seaforth's total casualties were 17 dead, 87 wounded and two missing.

INDIA AND BURMA
The Seaforth Highlanders, 1ˢᵗ battalion

At the outbreak of hostilities 1ˢᵗ Seaforth was still based in Shanghai as part of the international protection force, and it did not leave until August 1940. This time it did not return to Hong Kong but was sent to reinforce Malaya, where it was based in Penang. At the time there was a good deal of complacency about the defence of this strategically important colony and the huge naval base at Singapore. The prevailing view, put by Winston Churchill in a paper to the Cabinet in December 1939, while he was First Lord of the Admiralty, was that Singapore was an impregnable fortress and could be reduced only by a siege involving 50,000 men. As such, any potential enemy – probably Japan – would find it a difficult target to take:

> As Singapore is as far away from Japan as Southampton is from New York, the operation of moving a Japanese Army with all its troopships and maintaining it with men and munitions during a siege would be forlorn. Moreover such a siege, which would last at least four or five months, would be liable to be interrupted, if at any time Britain chose to send a superior fleet to the scene . . . It is not considered possible that the Japanese, who are a prudent people and reserve their strength for the command of the Yellow Sea and China, in which they are fully occupied, would embark on such a mad enterprise.

Events were to prove Churchill tragically wrong. On Sunday 7 December 1941 Japan entered the war with its infamous preemptive air strike on the US Pacific Fleet's base at Pearl Harbor in Hawaii. This was followed in quick succession by further Japanese attacks on the islands of Guam, Wake and Midway, while the Japanese Second Fleet escorted General Tomoyoku Yamashita's Twenty-Fifth Army to attack the north-west coast of the Malay peninsula. For the British this was a valuable asset as it produced almost 40 per cent of the world's rubber and 58 per cent of the world's tin; it was also the key to Britain's major naval base at Singapore. At the same time, three Japanese divisions prepared to invade the British colony of Hong Kong in southern China, a vital port and trading centre which had been in British hands since 1842. However, it was the collapse of Malaya and the surrender of Singapore on 15 February 1942 which caused the biggest dent to British pride and prestige in the region. Coupled with the concurrent invasion of Burma, the Japanese were suddenly in a position to threaten British interests in India, the 'Jewel in the Crown' of the country's imperial holdings.

By then 1st Seaforth had left Malaya for India and was spared the indignity of fighting in a campaign which brought little credit to the defending British, Indian and Australian forces and led to the capture of thousands of their men. There was also a lucky escape for the battalion's commanding officer, Lieutenant-Colonel R.A. Wolfe Murray, who had transferred to the reserve in January 1941 and was appointed liaison officer to the Local Defence Corps for Malaya. Sent to command a mixed force to defend the MacRitchie dam, he managed to avoid capture by escaping in a sampan which took him by way of the Dutch East Indies to Sumatra, where he was picked up by the Royal Australian Navy and returned to India. Between then and the end of the war he served in the Australian Army, latterly as commandant of the School of Infantry.

In March 1942 1st Seaforth was moved to Imphal on the Assam–Burma border following the beginning of the war with Japan; serving with 1st (Indian) Infantry Brigade in the 23rd (Indian)

Division, this was to be the battalion's area of operations for the next two and a half years. The bulk of the battalion's activities involved long-range patrolling in the Burmese jungle, often continuing operations during the heavy rains of the monsoon season. As a result casualties from malaria were high throughout the division in which 1st Seaforth was serving. In November 1942 the divisional commander, Lieutenant-General Ronald Savory, reported that his division was 5,000 troops short of its full complement of 17,000, a worrying consideration at a time when the Japanese forces were poised to attack the Imphal–Kohima area. Although invasion of India had not been part of the original intentions of the Japanese attack, their armed forces had won such a convincing victory in Burma that there seemed to be no reason why India should not fall equally cheaply. In July 1942 the Japanese high command made plans for 'Operation 21', a three-pronged attack from Burma towards Ledo, Imphal and Chittagong. It was over-ambitious, as the terrain in northern Burma was not suited to rapid offensive operations, but the fact that India was threatened was enough to concentrate British minds about the precariousness of their position. Allied to increasing demands from Indian nationalists for Britain to quit India was an immediate need to restore British standing by taking the offensive back to the Japanese and retrieving lost ground in Burma. The first of these initiatives was the first Arakan campaign, which opened in September 1942 and was aimed at capturing the Akyab peninsula following an advance from Chittagong by way of Cox's Bazaar and Donbaik. By the following May the Japanese had retrieved all the ground won during the advance; for the British it was not only an expensive failure which cost over 5,000 casualties, but it inculcated a belief that the Japanese were unbeatable jungle fighters. This was to be an important consideration in the fighting which lay ahead.

CHAPTER NINE

The Second World War 1943–45

The British victory at Alamein was not the end of the war but, as Churchill remarked at the time, it marked the beginning of the end. It was still the dark before the dawn and many problems lay ahead for the Allies in deciding the best way to prosecute the war. The shock of the Japanese attack suggested that the campaign in the Pacific should be given priority, but the strategic balance had changed. In addition to the losses in south-east Asia and the Pacific, command of the sea had also been surrendered and all that remained to the Allies was the Hawaii naval base, the garrison on Midway Island and the US carrier fleet which, fortuitously, had been at sea during the Japanese attack. There was an obvious American desire for retribution, but against that urgent need US war plans dictated a 'Germany first' policy. This was underscored at the first summit meeting between Roosevelt and Winston Churchill in Washington in December 1941, when the two leaders agreed that Germany would have to be defeated before they turned their attention to Japan. The conference also led to the establishment of the Combined Chiefs of Staff, composed of the British Chiefs of Staff and the American Joint Chiefs of Staff chaired by US General

George C. Marshall. Its first task was to begin the timetable for the invasion of Europe and to lay plans for a direct attack on Germany by invading France and driving quickly into Germany.

The opening of this second front would also take pressure off the Soviet Union, which had been invaded by German forces in the summer of 1941 and was fighting for its survival. In response to urgent requests for help from the Soviet leader, Joseph Stalin, Marshall put forward plans for a cross-Channel invasion as early as autumn 1942. Codenamed Sledgehammer, it would be launched against northern France but it would only take place if Germany appeared to be weakening or if the Soviet Union needed a diversionary attack to prevent an imminent collapse on the Eastern Front. Otherwise the invasion, codenamed Roundup, would take place the following spring. Marshall was bullish about both plans and believed that by attacking the heart of Germany the war would be shortened. Unless that happened, he argued, the Soviet Union would collapse and the war against Germany would last for a further decade and would require the creation of 200 divisions to win it. However, the British were unhappy with the plans, which General Sir Alan Brooke, chief of the imperial general staff, deemed reckless and likely to fail: 'The prospects of success are small and dependent on a mass of unknowns, whilst the chances of disaster are great.' Churchill also opposed the idea and had argued forcefully for a US invasion of North Africa which would trap German and Italian Axis forces under the command of General Erwin Rommel, engaged against the British Eighth Army in Libya and Egypt.

The clash between the rival plans put the coalition under immediate strain. Marshall thought that the campaign in the Mediterranean was a sideshow which would do nothing to dent the German war effort; only a direct attack on the German homeland would bring the war to an end. On the US side there were also fears that the British plan was aimed at propping up its imperial holdings –

the Mediterranean and the Suez Canal was the traditional route to India and the Far East and the presence of Rommel's forces had put it under threat. The stalemate had been broken by Roosevelt on 25 July 1942: Sledgehammer was cancelled; instead the immediate objective was North Africa, which was finally secured by the Allied victory in Tunisia. It was a momentous decision, which tied up a million US soldiers in a campaign which was the opposite of Marshall's plan to go straight for Germany's heart and led to the subsequent invasion of Sicily and Italy in the summer of 1943. At the same time, the British took the first steps in the long campaign to defeat the Japanese in Burma.

SICILY, ITALY AND GREECE
The Seaforth Highlanders, 2nd, 5th, 6th battalions
Queen's Own Cameron Highlanders, 2nd (new),
5th battalions, The Lovat Scouts

The next stage of the war against the Axis forces involved the capture of Sicily as a precursor to the invasion of peninsular Italy, a move which would lead to the final securing of the Mediterranean, with its vital maritime routes. Four Seaforth battalions, including The Seaforth Highlanders of Canada, were involved in the landings on Sicily, which began on 10 July 1943. In the initial assault phase the 6th battalion landed at Cassibile to the south of Syracuse and immediately came under heavy Italian machine-gun and artillery fire. Without fire support of its own, the battalion lost 40 casualties killed and wounded. Following the fall of Augusta the 5th Division pushed inland and 6th Seaforth was involved in the operations on the Simeto River and the Catania plain. In the second phase the Seaforth and Cameron battalions in 51st (Highland) Division came ashore from landing crafts on the beaches at Cape Passaro and moved quickly inland, where they first engaged the enemy at Francoforte on 14 July. From there they moved into the plain of Catania; while attacking the enemy airfields at Gerbini, 2nd Seaforth lost six officers and 74 soldiers killed, missing or wounded. On the night of 31 July, 5th Seaforth and 5th Camerons were involved in a successful brigade attack to capture enemy positions on the Sferro Hills. During the latter action the battalion lost five officers and 40 soldiers but had the satisfaction of taking 30 prisoners, and after the battle they buried 60 German and Italian dead.

While the operation had taken longer to complete than the Allies had planned, Sicily fell on 16 August. Some of the gloss was taken off the victory when over 100,000 German and Italian soldiers were evacuated across the Straits of Messina to fight again in Italy, but the battle for the island showed that British and US forces could work in tandem against a determined enemy. Before the culmination of the campaign 6th Seaforth was taken out of the line to refit and begin training with 5th Division for the next stage of the campaign in Italy, while the Seaforth and Cameron battalions in 51st (Highland) Division returned to Britain to start training for the long-awaited invasion of France. There was also a change of job for its experienced commander, Major-General Douglas Wimberley, who had led it so well in North Africa and Sicily: he was sent back to Britain to become commandant of the army staff college at Camberley. Before he left he issued an Order of the Day to All Ranks of the 51st Highland Division, thanking them for their 'spirit, discipline and behaviour' and reminding them that the member regiments could not rest on their laurels. He also included a verse which he felt summed up the spirit of the Highland soldier, be he a Scot from the Highlands or Lowlands, or one of the many Englishmen who had served in the division:

> Ye canna mak' a sojer wi' braid an' trappins braw,
> Nor gie him fightin' spirit when his backs ag'in the wa'.

It's the breedin' in the callants [young men] that winna let
them whine,
The bluid o' generations frae lang, lang syne.

The Allies followed up their successes with the invasion of Italy
in September 1943. At the same time the Italians decided to
surrender and while the Allies dithered over acceptance of the
terms the Germans moved 16 divisions into Italy to continue the
war, and these forces were to prove somewhat troublesome to the
Allies. For 6th Seaforth the invasion began on 3 September when
the main invasion force XIII Corps (5th Division, 1st Canadian
Division) crossed over to Italy, landing to the north of Reggio at
Gallico Marina. Meeting little resistance the battalion pushed up
through Calabria towards Potenza, to link up with the US Fifth
Army and British X Corps, which had landed at Salerno and had
immediately encountered determined German resistance. At the
end of the first week the 5th Division had moved 100 miles and
by 16 September had reached the Gulf of Policastro, where XIII
Corps was tasked with guarding the US Fifth Army's right flank.
During the next phase of the operation the 6th battalion moved
north from Foggia across the Trigno River into the highlands
around Vinchiaturo, where things became more difficult. Some of
the peaks were higher than Ben Nevis and the initial stages of the
attack were made in pitch dark and heavy rain.

The next stage of the advance took the battalion across the
River Moro to reach Lanciano, where it spent Christmas and the
New Year before pushing north again over the Garigliano. At the
crossing point the river was over 100 yards wide and the water
was found to be deep and swift-flowing. First the boats had to
be dragged up – 'an awkward and back-breaking job' – but as the
battalion War Diary reveals, the crossing, undertaken on the night
of 17 January, was equally difficult and dangerous:

D Company got across practically intact and started moving to the right, up the river bank. A Company was extending forward and to the left, in an attempt to contact B Company, landing from the sea. Headquarters embarked and crossed, and C Company assembled its boat crews and covering parties to be ferried over by 2nd Northamptons. D Company's progress could be followed as they mopped up the enemy posts. At one point, a German voice could be heard yelling and screaming, hysterically cursing the British and howling about the Fatherland. It stopped very suddenly.

Fortunately, the next target, the town of Argento, had been evacuated by the Germans before the division was ordered to take it 'at all costs'. Before being withdrawn from the Italian theatre of operations on 30 June, 5th Division served at the Anzio beachhead following the Allied landings and took part in the break-out which led ultimately to the fall of Rome. They then moved to Egypt prior to a posting in Palestine. By then 2nd Camerons had returned to the 4th Indian Division, which moved to Italy in February 1944. The Allied advance had been held up in the Liri Valley south of Rome, where the enemy resistance centred on the monastery at Monte Cassino, the mother-house of the Benedictine Order. It stood on high ground outside the town of the same name, which had been razed to the ground, and, being partially occupied by German forces, had become the scene of fierce fighting. The position fell on 17 May and as a result it opened up access to the valley of the River Liri and the coastal littoral, thus allowing the Allied infantry and armoured divisions to push north-east towards Rome. At the same time, on 23 May, US VI Corps broke out of the Anzio beach-head, having been bogged down there after the initial landings on 22 January. Rome fell to the US Fifth Army on 5 June and the Germans began a fighting retreat towards the Pisa–Rimini line, an operation in which 2nd Camerons played a full role. They also took part in the next phase of the Allied advance towards the Gothic Line in the Apennines to the north of Florence, stretching from Carrara in the west to Pesaro on the Adriatic in the east. According to one officer, quoted in the regimental records, the attack had been made 'over what must have been some of the most difficult and strongly defended country in the world'. In November, 2nd Camerons left Italy when 4th Indian Division was deployed to Greece as part of the peacekeeping forces following the withdrawal of the German army. By an odd coincidence they ended the war in the Struma Valley on the Salonika Front, the place that the same battalion had been stationed at the time of the Armistice in 1918.

No history of the campaigns in Sicily and Italy would be complete without mentioning the contribution made by other regiments with strong connections to The Seaforth Highlanders and Queen's Own Cameron Highlanders. In September 1939 The Lovat Scouts had mobilised and was deployed on coastal defence duties in the Faroe Islands before being trained as a mountain reconnaissance regiment. In that role it was sent to Italy, landing at Naples in July 1944 to serve with 10th Indian Division in the push towards the Gothic Line. At the end of the war The Lovat Scouts had reached Bologna and was subsequently deployed in Austria and Salonika, where it served with 4th Indian Division. The regiment was disbanded in October 1946. Also fighting in Italy was The Seaforth Highlanders of Canada, which served in 1st Canadian Division. This remarkable regiment was formed by 72nd Highlanders of Canada, which came into being in Vancouver in 1910 and served in the Canadian Expeditionary Force (CEF) on the Western Front during the First World War. In October 1944 the regiment received its first Victoria Cross, which was awarded to Private Ernest A. Smith for his courage in knocking out a German Mark V Panther tank and killing four Germans who counter-attacked his position. The Camerons also had Canadian affiliated regiments. The first, Queen's Own Cameron Highlanders of Canada, came into being in 1910 in Winnipeg, Manitoba, as 79th Cameron Highlanders of Canada. It served in the CEF in France and Flanders and formed part of the 3rd Canadian Division during the invasion of Europe in 1944 (see below). The second was The Cameron Highlanders of Ottawa. It was raised originally in 1861 as a militia regiment for home defence duties and following service in the First World War was redesignated The Cameron Highlanders of Ottawa in 1936. During the Second World War it served with 3rd Canadian Division as a machine-gun battalion and was awarded 20 battle honours during the fighting in France and north-west Europe.

BURMA
The Seaforth Highlanders, 1st battalion
Queen's Own Cameron Highlanders, 1st battalion

By the summer of 1943 the British and Indian armies had enjoyed their first successful offensive operation against the Japanese and in so doing had done much to alter the perception that the enemy was unbeatable. This was a result of the feats of a remarkable unit, 77th Indian Division, commanded by an equally remarkable soldier, Major-General Orde Wingate, an artillery officer who had previously served in Palestine, Ethiopia and Eritrea. The brigade (made up of so-called Chindits) had mounted a long-range penetration operation behind Japanese lines from February to April 1943. Operation Longcloth (as it was known) was a mixed success. It sowed confusion in the minds of the Japanese high command, who feared it was a precursor to a large attack and tied up troops to hunt down the Chindits. The Mandalay–Myitkyina railway line was cut but the cost was appalling. Of the 3,000 men who carried out the operation, only 2,182 came back; around 450 had been killed in action and the remainder were either lost or had been taken prisoner. Only 600 of the force were able to return to soldiering. Nevertheless Wingate had shown that the Japanese could be fought on their own terms and the Chindits were a huge propaganda success, so much so that a second, larger airborne operation was planned for the spring of 1944.

Wingate's operations were part of a wider offensive against the Japanese in 1944 and this involved 1st Seaforth and 1st Camerons, who had arrived in India in the summer of 1942. After a period of intensive training the latter battalion moved up to the Assam border as part of 2nd Division, which had been sent into the area in April 1944 when the Japanese under General Renya Mutaguchi opened a major offensive across the River Chindwin to attack Imphal and Kohima in Assam. This would give the Japanese the springboard to invade India and for that reason it was imperative for the British and Indian forces to hold not just those two key points but also the railhead at Dimapur, which was the end of the supply line from India. The orders were terse and to the point: open the road to Kohima and then recapture it. On 14 April, 1st Camerons took part in the first set-piece action to retake a position called Bunker Hill under the direction of Brigadier V.P.S. Hawkins, 5th Brigade, who left a vivid picture in the War Diary of the Camerons as they went into action:

> I spotted David Graham, one of the Company Commanders, walking about as if there were no Japs there and controlling his chaps magnificently. We actually saw him take a bullet through his shoulder and fall over as he was in the act of throwing a bomb. The actual attack went exactly as we hoped. There were no Japs on the back of the hill, and the Camerons were in full possession one half-hour after they first appeared. We afterwards counted 75 dead Japs on the position, and the total Cameron casualties were under 20.

After the battle Bunker Hill was christened Cameron Hill. From there the brigade fought its way towards Garrison Hill, the only part of Kohima garrisoned by Allied troops. This involved hard fighting against a determined enemy during which, according to one officer's account, the Camerons came 'to learn of the tenacity of the little Nip [Japanese soldier] and his amazing ability to do wonders in underground defence'. Kohima was eventually retaken on 25 June but at a cost: the casualties in the 1st battalion were six officers and 86 soldiers killed or missing and five officers and 186 soldiers wounded. The names of the dead are remembered on a memorial stone designed by Alan M'Killop, a Camerons' officer who had trained at Edinburgh College of Art. At the time of the fighting at Imphal and Kohima 1st Seaforth took part in operations which were designed to confuse the Japanese during the Chindits' airborne assault which began on 24 March. This involved an attack on the headquarters of the Japanese 15th Division at Kasom, and fresh impetus was provided by the rumour that the senior enemy commander was accompanied by his favourite geisha girls. This turned out not to be the case, but the position was taken on the night of 14/15 April, forcing the enemy to withdraw. By then the monsoon had begun and the Allies found themselves operating in conditions which tested their morale and their ingenuity. In the heavy rain tracks disappeared altogether, leaving impassable quagmires, food was often in short supply, malaria was an ever-present danger and the remaining pockets of Japanese resistance had to be cleared. An entry from the diary of Major R.D. Maclagan, 1st Seaforth (quoted in Colonel Sym's history), gives a good idea of the conditions soldiers had to endure during the monsoon:

> Rain, which had started at dawn, continued heavily and relentlessly all day. Conditions were extremely unpleasant. It was bitterly cold, particularly on Nippon Hill, which,

covered with craters and shell holes, was completely devoid
of any cover. Communication by wireless was hopeless, all
transmitting sets having long before gone out of commission
due to the intense rain.

It could have been a difficult phase but with the Japanese back on the
other side of the Chindwin there was the satisfaction of knowing that
the enemy had been defeated. The war in Burma was now entering
its final phase and the Allies decided on a twin assault which saw
General Sir William Slim's Fourteenth Army attack the enemy on
the line between Mandalay and Pakkoku (Operation Capital) while
a second amphibious and airborne assault on Rangoon was planned
at the beginning of 1945 (Operation Dracula). Slim's intention was
to break out from the Kohima area and to make a four-pronged
advance towards Indaw, Schwebo, Myinmu and Pakkoku. At the
same time Lieutenant-General Sir Philip Christison's XV Corps
would move into the Arakan and recapture the airfields, which
would extend Allied air cover to Rangoon and the border with
Thailand. The offensive opened on 3 December when the 11th East
African Division and the 20th Indian Division crossed the Chindwin
and began advancing with little sign of Japanese resistance. Faced by
less opposition than he had expected, Slim decided to feint towards
Mandalay while driving towards Meiktila, a key communications
centre. Once the upper reaches of the River Irrawaddy had been
seized, the way would be open to race south to Rangoon.

For the Camerons this meant taking part in 2nd Division's
move towards Schwebo, which had to be cleared before moving
on to Ywathitgyi on the River Irrawaddy. During the river crossing
on 24 February, 1st Camerons and 7th Worcesters formed the
bridgehead with 1st Royal Welch Fusiliers on the left flank and,
as recounted by Major I.J. Swanson in the regimental records, this
called for a good deal of ingenuity:

Rowing on a fast river wasn't the same as a stagnant pond; and some of our boats had already started going around in crazy circles. Somehow or other we settled down and paddling became a routine. The current was far stronger than had been calculated, but we seemed reasonably controlled, while overhead a Boston aircraft flew backwards and forwards to drown the noise of our oars.

The road to Rangoon lay ahead. Mandalay fell on 13 March while the 2nd Division, attacking from the west, captured Fort Ava. On 2 May the remaining Japanese were cut off in the Arakan and the next day the first units entered Rangoon following amphibious landings by the 26th Indian Division. For the Japanese in Burma the war was over and fighting came to an end in August following the dropping of atomic bombs on the cities of Hiroshima and Nagasaki. In September 1st Camerons moved to Japan as part of the Allied army of occupation while 1st Seaforth returned to India.

FRANCE AND NORTH-WEST EUROPE
The Seaforth Highlanders, 2nd, 5th, 6th, 7th battalions
Queen's Own Cameron Highlanders, 5th battalion

The decision to press ahead with the invasion of north-west Europe had been taken at the Allied conference in Washington in May 1943 and it was given the codename Overlord. The assault phase was codenamed Neptune, and planning for it began under joint US–British direction immediately after the summit had ended. The main desiderata for the cross-Channel amphibious attack were quickly established: a landing area with shallow beaches and without obstacles, which was within range of Allied air power; the neutralisation of local defences to allow a build-up which would equal the strength of the German defenders; and the presence of a large port for reinforcement and re-supply. Deception also formed part of the plan: the idea was to persuade the Germans that the assault would be made across the narrowest part of the English Channel at Pas de Calais, where the beaches were shallow and led into the hinterland without the obstacles of cliffs and high ground. It also offered the opportunity to make a quick strike into the Low Countries and from there into Germany. All those reasons made Pas de Calais the ideal place for invasion, but because it was the obvious location it was quickly discounted as the Allied planners knew that their German counterparts would deploy the bulk of their defensive forces there. By the end of the summer the plan was shown to the Allied leadership at the Quadrant conference in Quebec. The chosen landing ground was the Baie de la Seine in Normandy between Le Havre and the Cotentin peninsula, an area which met all the criteria, including a deepwater port at Cherbourg. Until it could be secured the Allies planned to use artificial harbours known as Mulberries, while fuel would be piped across the Channel through an under-sea pipeline known as Pluto.

The initial planning called for an invasion force of three divisions plus airborne forces which would create a bridgehead through which reinforcements could be landed quickly to break out into Normandy and Brittany. Success would depend on the ability of the Allies to build up forces more rapidly than the Germans, and with that in mind it would be essential to deny the enemy the chance to reinforce the landing grounds by destroying road and rail communications in northern France. Although Montgomery agreed with the main principles of the plan, he put forward an alternative proposal to attack in greater weight, along a broader front and with a larger airborne contribution. This was backed by Eisenhower, who activated his headquarters in February. It was agreed that the initial assault should be made by five divisions, two US, two British and one Canadian, with one British and two US airborne divisions operating on the flanks. The D-Day invasion began on 6 June with the airborne forces securing the flanks overnight while the main assault went in at dawn, preceded by a mighty bombardment from 2,000 warships in the Channel. By the end of the day the assault divisions were ashore and the five landing areas – codenamed Utah, Omaha, Gold, Sword and Juno – had been secured with around 10,000 Allied casualties (killed, wounded and missing), fewer than expected.

For the two regiments the invasion of northern Europe brought a mixture of experiences, although all the battalions fought in the same operations and were frequently in the line at the same time. The battalions serving in the 51st (Highland) Division were part of the second wave of the invasion force which landed in France between 7 and 9 June. Their first task was to secure the Orne bridgehead, which had been captured by airborne forces and which the Germans desperately wanted to retake. Some idea of the ferocity of the fighting can be seen in the events of 23 June when 17 tanks were destroyed on the front held by 2nd and 5th Seaforth and 5th Camerons. By then 7th Seaforth had arrived in France as part of 15th (Scottish) Division and found themselves involved in heavy fighting against German positions on the Eterville Ridge south of Odon where enfilading fire caused heavy casualties. While the battalions were pinned down on the reverse slopes of the ridge on 11 July their War Diary recorded an unusual incident involving the rival Scottish and German mortar teams:

> During the action a voice came on the Mortar Officer's set – 'You think you can shoot, see how German mortars shoot', and a stonk [round of mortar shells] landed all around him. 'Are you still there? Good shooting, yes?' Back went the answer: '------- awful, is this better?' and stonked four likely spots. No more was heard.

A week later, following a massive aerial bombardment on the German positions, Operation Goodwood was launched with the intention of breaking out towards Caen. For 5th Seaforth this meant taking part in an attack on the Triangle, a wooded area to the east of Escoville. During the assault they were backed up by Crocodile flame-throwing tanks and succeeded in taking all the targets assigned to them. Eighty Germans were taken prisoner – some of them were Poles and Russians – and the battalion's losses were 11 killed and 51 wounded. Following the early breakthrough the Allied attack faltered and for the next ten days the two Seaforth battalions and 5th Camerons were pinned down around the Triangle, where they endured a torrid time from German bombers and the local mosquito population. Alastair Borthwick, now the Intelligence Officer of 5th Seaforth, reckoned that on average each man had approximately 20 stings on each hand and the 'darkness brought multistrikes'.

After the failure of the Goodwood attack it became clear that 51st (Highland) Division had lost much of its fighting spirit due to exhaustion and the strain of being constantly in action, with the attendant high rate of casualties. When Lieutenant-Colonel (later Lieutenant-General Sir) Derek Lang took over command of 5th Camerons at the end of July he was their fifth commanding officer in seven weeks. So serious was the fall in morale that in mid-July Montgomery reported to the chief of the imperial general staff that the 51st (Highland) Division was no longer 'battleworthy' and 'does not fight with determination'. One Cameron officer quoted in the divisional history could see morale seeping away from the men as they faced a constant diet of enemy fire:

> Nothing was easier in a night attack, but to stop, tie a bootlace and disappear. In Normandy this became more and more prevalent. We dealt with this in a number of ways; no breakfast for a start; no NAAFI [Navy, Army, Air Force

Institute] rations (i.e. no cigarettes) for a week; a threat to inform their next of kin of their behaviour. The scorn of their peers was also a very effective deterrent. I had one Jock in Normandy who was marched into battle with a bayonet up his backside.

As a result of this widespread slump in morale, which could have been disastrous for every regiment in 51st (Highland) Division, Montgomery was forced to sack its commander, Major-General Charles Bullen-Smith, late of the King's Own Scottish Borderers, who had succeeded Wimberley, on the grounds that 'the men won't fight for you'. It was a drastic move to make in the middle of a battle but although Montgomery was loath to make it he had no option. Bullen-Smith was replaced by Major-General T.G. Rennie, a former commanding officer of 5th Black Watch.

At the same time the division was taken out of the line for a short period of rest and recuperation at Cazelle, north-west of Caen, and some of the under-strength battalions were reinforced with fresh soldiers, many of them from English regiments. Ahead lay Operation Totalise, a thrust out of Caen towards Falaise mounted by the Canadian First Army with 51st (Highland) Division in support. Before the attack, which began on 8 August, Rennie reminded his senior officers that it could be 'the decisive battle in France' and that he expected every soldier in the division to show the same 'determination and offensive spirit' that they had demonstrated at Alamein. Although the Germans put up stout resistance Falaise fell on 16 August and the way to the River Seine was open. By then the 51st (Highland) Division had returned to its old form despite being the victim of 'friendly fire' from RAF strike aircraft. In one incident in mid-August the battalion headquarters of 5th Camerons was attacked by five Spitfires even though yellow recognition panels were displayed.

Fortunately no one was killed, but various vehicles and radio sets were destroyed.

The next problem for the Allies was overstretch – as they moved away from the beachheads their supply lines became longer and that had an impact on the speed of their advance into north-west Europe. It also meant that the war would not end in 1944. In September the Highland Division took part in the operation to take the ports of Le Havre and Dunkirk and this was followed by a highly emotional moment when St Valéry was retaken amidst scenes of great local jubilation. For Colonel Lang it was an especially poignant experience. He had been adjutant of 4th Camerons in 1940 but had managed to escape; now he was being welcomed by the mayor in the town square. From there the advance took the division into Flanders and on into Holland where the flat 'polder' lowlands had been flooded, causing inevitable problems. During the same phase 7th Seaforth had crossed the Seine south of Rouen with the rest of 15th (Scottish) Division and had advanced into Belgium by way of Loos and Courtrai, stark reminders of the earlier conflict. This included a period of intensive fighting as the division fought its way over a succession of formidable water obstacles towards the River Maas.

It was at this stage of the battle, when the Allies were still confident that the end of the war was in sight and when conditions were at their worst, that the Germans decided to counter-attack in the Ardennes. The plan was the brainchild of Adolf Hitler, who reasoned as early as September that the winter weather – 'night, fog and snow' – would give the Germans the opportunity to hit back at the Allies through the dense Ardennes forest, with its narrow steep-sided valleys, and then turn rapidly north to recapture Brussels and Antwerp. The attack would split the Allies, leaving the US armies unable to come to the aid of Montgomery's 21st Army Group which would be encircled and destroyed before it could attack the Ruhr.

It did not turn out that way but the Battle of the Bulge, as it came to be known, almost allowed the Germans to achieve their aims by creating a huge salient or 'bulge' in the Allied lines. During the successful Allied counter-offensive 51st (Highland) Division came under US command during an attack on Laroche. As Andrew Todd recalled in his war history of 2nd Seaforth, fierce German fighting and the bitterly cold winter weather made the Battle of the Bulge a grim experience for everyone who took part in it:

> Deep snow covered the countryside. In the rolling hills and glens, movement by wheeled vehicles was possible only on the roads, where the snow became dappled with the blue spots of anti-freeze. The narrow tracked Bren carriers were totally unmanageable. Even the tanks rarely strayed from the tarmac surfaces.

Ahead lay the equally ferocious fighting in the Reichswald, which housed part of the Siegfried Line, the heavily fortified German defensive position. The 51st (Highland) Division's objective was the town of Goch, which had to be taken to secure the southern sector of the Reichswald in preparation for the crossing of the Rhine. It was a hard-fought battle which involved close-quarter fighting and, according to those who were on the receiving end, the heaviest enemy bombardment since Alamein. The fall of Goch and another strongpoint at Hekkens opened the way for the Rhine crossing, which began on 23 March 1945. The two assault divisions were 15th (Scottish) and 51st (Highland); all the Scottish battalions got safely across the river but during the operation the 51st (Highland) Division suffered a setback when General Rennie was killed during a heavy German mortar attack near the town of Rees. It was a shattering blow as Rennie had been a popular and inspiring commander. He was succeeded by Major-General

Gordon Macmillan, an experienced and well-liked Argyll and Sutherland Highlander.

Once across the river the Scottish battalions found that the German defenders were in no mood to surrender and some units seemed to fight with a greater fanaticism as they fell back on the 'Fatherland'. During the 2nd Seaforth's action at Rees, the ruined town proved to be 'a tough nut' which involved a good deal of house-to-house fighting before it fell. The 5th Seaforth had a similar experience at Groin, which Alastair Borthwick described as 'the hardest village fight the Battalion ever fought', while the abiding memory for 7th Seaforth was the horror of the Nazi concentration camp at Celle, an overflow of Belsen, which only made 'determination grimmer'. There was equally tough fighting at Isselburg for 5th Camerons, and its final action was at Glinde during the advance to Bremerhaven. Nevertheless, the Rhine crossing was the beginning of the end and for the next month the 51st (Highland) Division was constantly on the move as it fought its way north towards Bremen and Bremerhaven, where a victory parade was held on 12 May. It had been a hard-won victory: from 1939 to the end of the war 51st (Highland) Division had lost 16,469 casualties, 3,084 of them killed in action. The 6th Seaforth also ended the war in north Germany. After being withdrawn from Italy it refitted in Egypt and served with 5th Division, which landed at Marseilles in March 1945 before advancing north towards the Elbe.

CHAPTER TEN

Cold War and
Counter-Insurgency

At the end of the war against Nazi Germany, Italy and Japan, Britain's armed forces were scattered around the world. The war also left the country exhausted, physically and economically, and inevitably there was a good deal of retrenchment. Fighting the war had cost the country £3,000 million and there remained a high level of debt arising from loans made by the US during and after the conflict; exports had fallen to new levels and sterling was weak. Industry, too, was in turmoil as the incoming Labour government introduced a rapid policy of nationalisation of coal-mining, the railways and steel. Inevitably, the armed forces were not immune from the adverse economic conditions. Just over five million men and women were still in uniform and the army alone had 20 divisions, but it quickly became clear that the cost of maintaining those forces was beyond the reach of a country whose economy had been devastated. As a result, cutbacks and scaling-down became the order of the day. By 1951 the size of the infantry had shrunk to 20 per cent of the army's total size – 88,100 soldiers out of a total strength of 417,800 – all line-infantry regiments had been reduced to a single battalion, wartime Territorial battalions had been scrapped or amalgamated and the combat units had fallen to 184, consisting of 77 infantry battalions, eight Gurkha battalions, 69 artillery regiments and 30 armoured regiments. The specialist corps – the Royal Engineers, the Royal Electrical and Mechanical Engineers, the Royal Army Service Corps, the Royal Army Ordnance Corps – had all expanded during the war and would remain dominant in the peacetime army. At the same time expenditure on the army was also reduced from £350 million to £270 million and Second World War equipment was not replaced in any quantity until the 1950s, forcing Field Marshal Viscount Montgomery of Alamein, chief of the imperial general staff between 1946 and 1948, to remark that 'the army was in a parlous condition, and was in a complete state of unreadiness and unpreparedness for war'.

At the same time the country retained many of its pre-war strategic obligations and needed soldiers on the ground to maintain them. The scale of the commitments meant that manpower became a problem for all three services, especially for the army, which was in danger of being overstretched. The government had a commitment to demobilise war-service men and women but at the same time it needed trained soldiers for a wide variety of tasks. Wartime legislation for conscription was therefore kept in place and under a succession of National Service Acts every male citizen was obliged to register at his local branch of the Ministry of Labour and National Service as soon as he became 18. Between the end of the war and the phasing out of conscription in 1963, 2.3 million men served as National Servicemen, the majority in the army. In its final form the period of conscription was two years following two earlier periods of 12 and 18 months and like every other regiment in the British Army, The Seaforth Highlanders and Queen's Own Cameron Highlanders benefited from the contribution made by men who were the first peacetime conscripts in British history.

Some of them undoubtedly enjoyed their time in the armed forces, learned a trade, passed their driving tests or travelled abroad for the first time in their lives. A few gained commissions; others just liked service life and, like Private Alexander Robb, 1st Seaforth, enjoyed the companionship of barrack life and the character training that came with pride and discipline:

> We had three super instructors, Sergeant Rennie, Corporal Le Page and Corporal Baker, who were very strict but fair to all. Sergeant Rennie told us that he had never had a squad win the passing-out parade at the end of six weeks' training – at Redford Barracks in Edinburgh there were six Highland regiments, HLI, Argylls, Seaforths, Black Watch, Camerons and Gordons. As none of us had much money, around £1 a week, Saturday was the only day any of us went out, either to Tynecastle or Easter Road to watch football, then a fish supper and a stroll round the centre of Edinburgh before the tram back to Redford. We all decided we would try our best not to let Sergeant Rennie down. We used to practise what we had learned during the day in barrack-room after cleaning our kit. On the two passing-out days we won the cross-country run, weapon-training, PT, turn-out and drill and came second in shooting. First overall. As we sat at our passing-out meal – of course we were at the top table – it gave us all satisfaction to see Sergeant Rennie's face completely light up, as proud as Punch.

Of course, in contrast, there are also former National Servicemen who have somewhat different memories of bullying NCOs, indifferent food, the loss of liberty and counting the days to demob, but as with so many other things in life it all depended on what the individual was prepared to put into the experience.

THE SEAFORTH HIGHLANDERS

The end of the war found the 1st battalion in India training for Operation Zipper to invade Malaya, and although the Japanese surrender meant that the invasion went ahead unopposed there was still a need to send troops to the country to restore law and order. This was followed by a short deployment in Java where Indonesian nationalists were attempting to overthrow Dutch rule. In October 1946 the battalion returned to Malaya under the command of Lieutenant-Colonel J.S.H. Douglas to be stationed first at Ipoh and then at Singapore. For the 2nd battalion there was a return to Britain in 1946 and postings to Warminster and then Bicester. Shortly after its return the regiment's fate had been settled. In common with the other line-infantry regiments of the British Army, The Seaforth Highlanders was forced to reduce its size to one battalion through the amalgamation of its 1st and 2nd battalions, with the latter being placed 'in suspended animation'. This allowed the old 2nd battalion to be run down and for those remaining to join the 1st battalion in Malaya. At the same time the three Territorial battalions (5th, 6th and 7th) were disbanded in the autumn of 1946 but the following year 11th Seaforth Highlanders (TA) was formed with company headquarters across the regiment's traditional recruiting area.

The Seaforth Highlanders returned to Malaya at a difficult time. During the Second World War the country had been overrun and captured by the Japanese army, which then garrisoned it with 100,000 troops. The only opposition came from mainly Malay-Chinese guerrilla groups, which mounted a limited number of attacks against Japanese installations with the support of Force 136, a British-backed counter-insurgency group. At the end of the war this Malayan People's Anti-Japanese Army was transformed into the Malayan Races Liberation Army (MRLA), which was the military wing of the Chinese-controlled Malayan Communist

Party (MCP). Initially Britain planned a Malayan Union which would have given the Chinese citizenship rights, but this was opposed by the Malay political elite and the result was the creation of a Malayan Federation in which Chinese rights were sacrificed to the interests of the Malay rulers. As a result of the heightened political tensions the Chinese Communists' opposition turned into an armed struggle in 1948, the MCP was declared illegal and some 10,000 MRLA fighters moved into the jungle to mount guerrilla operations against the civilian population and the security forces under their military commander Chin Peng.

Initially the idea was to drive the terrorists (known as CTs, for 'Communist Terrorists') into the jungle away from urban populations, but this changed in April 1950 with the appointment of Lieutenant-General Sir Harold Briggs as director of operations 'to plan, co-ordinate and to direct the anti-bandit operations of the police and fighting services'. To achieve those ends Briggs integrated the efforts of the police and the military, and reorganised the intelligence services to provide him with information about terrorist movements and infiltrate the Communist cadre infrastructure. A 'food denial' policy was also instituted but the main obstacle was the support given to the MRLA by the Chinese inhabitants of the jungle. The solution was the resettlement of 650,000 villagers in 550 New Villages – secure areas where, it was hoped, they would enjoy a safe and profitable environment away from MRLA influence. Then it was the task of the infantry to move into the jungle, to secure bases and drive the CTs into the deeper and less hospitable depths. As the men of 1st Seaforth discovered – the description below comes from an account of a jungle patrol in Colonel Sym's history – these operations demanded strength, stamina and determination, and only the very fittest were able to withstand the rigours of the environment:

Sleeping in the jungle, you become aware of how noisy it is, with the chirp of crickets, the twittering of birds at night, and the loud whistling of frogs. Small animals rustle among the leaves, and every now and then, a rotten branch falls, or a forest giant, eaten away by ants, crashes to earth. In contrast to the heat and sweat of toiling on the march, the night air becomes chilly as the moisture of the clothes dries out.

During the deployment in Malaya the battalion was based first in Johore and then eastern and central Pahang. While patrolling in the jungle the first thing that struck the men of 1st Seaforth was its frighteningly large scale. The trees, forming an unbroken canopy, often reached 200 feet, their leaves sometimes as large as warrior's shields; and all around the base crazy patterns of creepers and roots constructed obstacles that were well-nigh impassable but for brute force and razor-sharp parangs or machetes. Underfoot, rotting leaves and undergrowth produced a soft mushy surface frequently traversed by meandering streams which turned what footholds there were into a spongy swamp. Then there was the fighting against the CTs: usually short-lived and unexpected firefights against a determined enemy. To help underline the idea that on one level the war was an impersonal activity, each battalion kept a score-sheet of terrorists killed – 1st Seaforth accounted for just under 100. Its own casualties were five officers and nine soldiers killed in action and five officers and 14 soldiers wounded.

The battalion's deployment in Malaya came to an end in the spring of 1951, when it returned to Edinburgh for a two-year posting. Its next move was to Buxtehude in West Germany to join 31 Lorried Infantry Brigade in the 7th Armoured Division as part of the British Army of the Rhine (BAOR). With the creation of the North Atlantic Treaty Organisation (NATO) in September

1949, BAOR was allotted to this new defensive alliance and the Northern Army Group in Germany (plus Norway and Denmark) came under the command of British generals. This was Britain's contribution to the post-war defence of western Europe and in some respects Germany was to take over India's role in the affections of generations of post-war British servicemen. In the first years the rationale for being in post-war Germany, by then divided into West and East, was not always apparent to soldiers but following the blockade of Berlin in 1948 the confrontation between NATO and the Soviet Union became increasingly bitter and belligerent. In time the period would be known as the Cold War and for the rest of the century West Germany was to be a second home for the regiment, as it was for every other regiment in the British Army.

Following a brief return to Scotland in May 1954, when it was based at Elgin, the place where the 72nd Highlanders had been raised in 1778, 1st Seaforth moved to the Suez Canal Zone. Of all the postings on offer to the post-war serviceman, this was the most unpopular and it left an indelible mark on all who served there: the fly-blown, sand-strewn military bases in the Zone were forlorn and disagreeable, the climate was vile and the local population was hostile. The Zone had been created during the Second World War and in March 1947 it had become a secure base for the British Army following nationalist protests at the British military presence in Egypt. (British forces remained in the country as 'guests' following a treaty signed in 1936.) By the time 1st Seaforth arrived the British garrisons were locked into the Zone, ostensibly guarding the Suez Canal but in effect protecting themselves from outraged Egyptian nationalists including the Bulak Nizam, paramilitary auxiliaries who had mastered the hit-and-run tactics of guerrilla warfare. In 1952 the atmosphere had worsened when the pro-British King Farouk was deposed and replaced with a military council headed by Major-General Mohammed Neguib. Two years later there was further change when Colonel Gamal Abdul Nasser, a perfervid Egyptian nationalist, seized power and served notice on Britain to quit the Zone within 20 months. During 1ˢᵗ Seaforth's time in the Zone the headquarters of Middle East Land Forces was in the process of transferring to Cyprus and the battalion's duties included the provision of guards for installations and internal security duties.

At the end of the deployment in June 1955 the battalion was sent at short notice to Aden to support the Aden Protectorate Levies (the British-officered local defence force) in a counter-insurgency campaign against dissident tribesmen who had been encouraged by Nasser's increasingly strident rhetoric to rebel against British rule. Aden and its surrounding protectorates had been in British hands since the previous century – the Red Sea port of Aden was considered to be an important strategic base for protecting oil supplies from the Persian Gulf – and Britain was determined to retain its influence in the area. However, control of the port was dependent on the protectorate states in the hinterland and in 1955 tribal rebellions in the Western Aden Protectorate (WAP) had been fomented into a nationalist uprising which was given military support by the neighbouring Imam of Yemen, Ahmad bin Yahya. At the time the failure to stop the supply of arms into WAP was considered an inconvenience, but it was to have major repercussions for the colony during the next 12 years (see below). Towards the end of 1955, 1ˢᵗ Seaforth moved to Gibraltar, another important strategic base, and it was to be their home until October 1957, when the battalion transferred to Münster as part of 6 Brigade in the British 2ⁿᵈ Division. By then the regiment's future lay in amalgamation with Queen's Own Cameron Highlanders (see below) and the farewell parade was held on 25 November 1960 in Münster, the salute being taken by the colonel of the regiment, General Sir James Cassels, a distinguished

Seaforth soldier, later to be promoted field marshal and to serve as chief of the general staff between 1965 and 1968.

QUEEN'S OWN CAMERON HIGHLANDERS

Between 1946 and 1947 1st Camerons had been deployed on internal security duties in Japan following the country's capitulation to the Allies. The battalion's base was at Hiro on Shikoku Island to the south of Hiroshima, one of the two cities which had been devastated by the dropping of atomic bombs in August 1945. The next posting was to Ipoh in Malaya in February 1947, and the battalion returned to Edinburgh in April 1948, just as the 'emergency' (as it was known at the time) was about to break out. Their move back to Scotland coincided with the disbandment of the 2nd battalion under the post-war reductions to the size of the army. Following service in Greece the 2nd battalion had moved to Klagenfurt in Austria, where it formed part of the post-war garrison before moving to northern Italy. It returned to Britain from Trieste in September 1947 and was disbanded on 30 June 1948 (first raised in 1804, it had been disbanded in 1815 and then re-raised in 1897). As happened on earlier similar occasions, the disbandment allowed the 1st battalion to be reinforced. In the Territorial Army 4/5th Camerons remained in being, with companies based in Inverness, Badenoch, Lochaber and Skye, Uist and Nairn.

The first deployment for the new 1st battalion was to Tripoli, to join 1st Guards Brigade. An important strategic base for Allied interests during the Second World War, Tripoli was the seat of the British military administration which ruled the former Italian colonies of Tripolitana and Cyrenaica until they became independent in 1951 as the United Kingdom of Libya under the supervision of the United Nations (UN). During this relatively quiet posting the battalion provided reinforcements for other Scottish regiments serving in Malaya or fighting in the war in South Korea, where

British servicemen had been sent in September 1950 to support a US-led UN army following the invasion of the country by its northern neighbour. Shocked by the aggression, Washington had persuaded the UN to oppose the invasion and Britain had added to the four US divisions with a weakened brigade group which took part in the desperate defence of the Pusan Perimeter in the south-east corner of the country. As the war progressed, though, and Chinese 'volunteers' came to the assistance of North Korea, the reasons for the UN involvement blurred and the fighting became a stalemate of entrenched positions and artillery barrage as the rival armies fought it out while the politicians argued about ways of resolving the conflict. The fighting did not come to an end in July 1953, when a truce was signed, and as the Camerons were to discover, a British military presence was required in the country until well into the decade.

Before that happened, in November 1951 the 1st battalion was sent at short notice to the Suez Canal Zone, where it was based at the ordnance depot at Tel-el-Kebir, scene of the battle against Egyptian insurgents in 1882 in which the regiment had played a leading role (see Chapter Five). The deployment coincided with a large-scale reinforcement of 6,000 soldiers to deal with an outbreak of local rioting following the decision of the Egyptian prime minister, Nahas Pasha, to abrogate the treaty of 1936 (see above), giving the British the legal right to station a garrison in the Zone. The Egyptians responded to the move by withdrawing all civilian labour from the Zone and instigating a terrorist campaign led by the Bulak Nizam. British civilian and military personnel and their families came under attack and as the violence escalated, the battalion spent most of its time guarding the base. In January 1952 the GOC Middle East Lieutenant-General Sir George Erskine ordered an offensive against suspected Bulak Nizam positions in Ismailia, but the operation was not a complete success. At least 40 Egyptian policemen were killed and in Cairo British property was burned down by way of retaliation. Three months later 1st Camerons left Port Said and returned to Edinburgh for a short tour of public duties before moving to Spittal an der Drau in Austria, where it joined the garrison in the British-controlled zone of the country. This was considered to be a plum posting – food and drink were not in short supply and the Alpine landscape made a pleasing backdrop – and the country was to be the battalion's home until November 1953, when it moved north to Lüneburg in West Germany to join 31 Lorried Infantry Brigade in 7th Armoured Division.

West Germany had become familiar territory for the British soldier. The British zone of occupation was in the north and included the industrial Ruhr as well as the port of Hamburg and the open spaces of the Lüneburg Heath. Immediately after the war the British adopted a strict policy of non-fraternisation which was summed up by the warning in a contemporary army handbook:

> You are about to meet a strange people in a strange enemy country. When you meet the Germans you will probably think they are very much like us. They look like us except there are fewer of the wiry type and more big fleshy types.

However, by the time the Camerons arrived the rules had been relaxed and during the National Service years of the 1950s there were ample possibilities to visit the local towns, with their pubs and cafés. Four British divisions were stationed there – 2nd Infantry, 6th Armoured, 7th Armoured and 11th Armoured – and the headquarters of British 1st Corps was at Rheindahlen, five miles outside München-Gladbach. In 1955, the year that 1st Camerons left Lüneburg, the Federal Republic of Germany was permitted to become a full member of NATO, to re-arm and thereby to make a full contribution to Western defence.

The battalion's next deployment was to South Korea as part of 1st Commonwealth Division, but before it left for the Far East there was a short stay at Elgin between February and July 1955. By then the war had been over for two years, but there was still a need to maintain a defensive posture to discourage any thoughts of further North Korean or Chinese aggression and the battalion occupied prepared positions south of the Imjin River, scene of some of the fiercest fighting of the earlier war. Amongst the responsibilities was the need to patrol the Demilitarised Zone along the 38th parallel, which remained an unquiet place with shootings and invasion threats in spite of the Armistice. In August 1953 the US entered into a mutual defence treaty with South Korea and built up a substantial garrison in the country; when the Commonwealth Division was disbanded 1st Camerons came under US command for a short time. Before leaving the country in the summer of 1956 the battalion trained in jungle warfare and counter-insurgency operations in preparation for a move to Malaya but the deployment was cancelled due to a crisis which had erupted over President Nasser's decision to take control of the Suez Canal, a move which not only hit British prestige but forced all ships using the Canal to pay fees to the Egyptian government and not to the British–French consortium which owned the canal.

On 27 July, the day after Nasser's proclamation, Britain's prime minister, Anthony Eden, asked the chiefs of staff to prepare plans for an invasion and recapture of the Canal in conjunction with French forces. Among the many problems encountered were uncertainty about the legality of going to war with Egypt, the overstretch of the armed forces and the difficulty of creating a workable plan for an operation on which there was no common agreement. From the outset the plans were fraught with problems and offensive operations did not begin until the first week of November, following a successful Israeli attack on Sinai. With British complicity France had brought Israel into the plan and encouraged its forces to attack across the Sinai Desert towards the Canal. This allowed France and Britain to emerge as peacemakers by issuing an ultimatum to both countries to stop fighting and remove their forces from the vicinity of the Canal or face the consequences of military intervention. As had been anticipated, it was an undertaking which Nasser could not accept and the next phase saw Allied air attacks on Egyptian bases to destroy the Egyptian air force, while British and French airborne forces landed on 5 November, seized their objectives at Gamil and Port Fuad without much difficulty and paved the way for a seaborne landing at Port Said. All Egyptian resistance was quashed by 6 November but by then the 'war' was over before it had begun. Soviet belligerency and US financial pressure forced Eden to call a ceasefire and to turn the problem over to the United Nations. It was a humiliating moment, yet Britain had no option but to comply as Washington had refused to support Britain's application to the International Monetary Fund for a loan to support the falling pound unless these conditions were met.

While those events were unfolding the Camerons were bound not for Egypt but for Aden, where there had been a dramatic escalation in anti-British feeling caused both by the Suez operation and by the continuing incursions over the border with Yemen. The importance of the Aden base had been reinforced by the Suez debacle and the British government was determined to hold on to it, even if that meant ruling out any move towards self-government in the foreseeable future. The battalion's duties included internal security and patrolling the protectorate's border with Yemen. Shortly before the battalion left the colony in March 1958 there was a further escalation in the violence with a number of grenade attacks against British targets and the governor William Luce was forced to declare a state of emergency. On its return to Britain the battalion was the last infantry regiment to be based in the historic barracks at Dover Castle and early in 1960 it moved to Edinburgh prior to the amalgamation with The Seaforth Highlanders as part of the reduction of the army. As its new partner had done, the regiment arranged a number of ceremonial events: its colours were laid up in Glasgow Cathedral and the farewell parade took place in Edinburgh on 25 November 1960, with the salute being taken by the colonel of the regiment, Major-General Douglas Wimberley, the much revered wartime commander of the 51st (Highland) Division.

QUEEN'S OWN HIGHLANDERS (SEAFORTH AND CAMERONS)

Following the announcement of the end of National Service as part of the Conservative government's defence review in 1957 – the last National Serviceman did not in fact leave the army until May 1963 – the army began to draw down its size to 185,000 soldiers. As a result, 30 regiments were ordered to amalgamate and under the terms of an Army Council directive of 13 June 1957 it was agreed that two of the pairings should be made in Scotland, one each from the Highland and Lowland Brigades. At the time the infantry had been reorganised for administrative purposes with the creation of three 'category' brigades (Guards, Light Infantry and Green Jacket) and 11 'regional' brigades. For Scotland the latter were the Lowland Brigade (Royal Scots, Royal Scots Fusiliers, King's Own Scottish Borderers, Cameronians) and the Highland Brigade (Black Watch, Highland Light Infantry, Seaforth Highlanders, Queen's Own Cameron Highlanders, Gordon Highlanders, Argyll and Sutherland Highlanders). The colonels of both brigades then met at Scottish Command in Edinburgh on 26 June. The Highland colonels decided that The Highland Light Infantry should remain in the brigade and that two Highland regiments should be amalgamated, the choice falling on The Seaforth Highlanders and Queen's Own Cameron Highlanders to form the Queen's Own Highlanders. At the same time the Lowland colonels met and recommended that The Royal Scots Fusiliers should amalgamate with The Highland Light Infantry.

The two Lowland regiments mounted well-orchestrated (but ultimately unsuccessful) campaigns to prevent the amalgamation but it went ahead as planned in 1959, the new regiment being known as The Royal Highland Fusiliers. However, the 'marriage' between the two Highland regiments proceeded relatively smoothly and harmoniously; the amalgamation took place at Redford Barracks in Edinburgh on 7 February 1961 when 1st Seaforth and 1st Camerons combined to become 1st Queen's Own Highlanders. Two months later the new battalion sailed for Singapore, where it joined 99 Gurkha Infantry Brigade on internal security duties. During the deployment 1st Queen's Own Highlanders was involved in suppressing a pro-Indonesian rebellion against the Sultan of Brunei led by 4,000 insurgents under the control of Yassin Effendi. This had been fomented by President Ahmed Sukarno of Indonesia, who was opposed to the British-backed creation of a Malaysian Federation of which Brunei would have been a member. The revolt flared up on 8 December 1962 and initially Effendi and his followers enjoyed some success, capturing a number of outlying towns including Seria, Tutong and Limbang. His failure to take the main airport and the sultan's palace proved to be decisive. Two days later the first British units from Singapore started arriving by sea and by air – the battalion's B Company was transported on board the destroyer HMS *Cavalier* – and within six days of their arrival the rebellion had collapsed. The battalion played a major role in retaking Anduki airfield and clearing rebels from Seria, where A Company was flown in by five Twin Pioneer aircraft. After taking part in the mopping-up operations the battalion returned to Singapore in February 1963 on board the Commando carrier HMS *Albion*.

For the next two decades the battalion's experiences were to be dominated by two factors: commitment to BAOR in Germany and eight periods of service in Northern Ireland on internal security duties following outbreaks of sectarian violence in Belfast and Londonderry in August 1969. Each tour of the province brought its own challenges in helping to keep the peace and maintain a sense of proportion in one of the most difficult and long-lasting counter-insurgency wars fought by the British Army. The main opponents were the Provisional Irish Republican Army but trouble was also fomented by Unionist terrorist groups and others. The period also included two tours of duty in Belize to defend the colony (formerly British Honduras) from the threat of attack from neighbouring Honduras, a deployment to Sharjah in 1969–70 to protect British oil interests in the Trucial States, a spell in Hong Kong as the resident battalion between March 1980 and December 1981 and a controversial involvement in the Falklands War of 1982.

Following Argentina's invasion to capture the Falkland Islands in April 1982 Britain responded by despatching a task force which included 3 Commando Brigade and, latterly, 5 Infantry Brigade. As the Spearhead battalion on instant readiness for service anywhere in the world, 1st Queen's Own Highlanders was well placed to take part in the operation and was twice placed on stand-by, but to widespread bemusement within the army it was not used. Its eventual task was to lead the operations in restoring normality to the islands once the Argentine forces had been defeated and expelled. For the battalion's work in Port Stanley and the outlying settlements the regiment was presented with the prestigious Wilkinson Sword of Peace.

In March 1988 the battalion moved back to Germany, again to Münster where it formed part of 6 Armoured Brigade equipped with the AFV-432 tracked fighting vehicle capable of carrying a section into battle. Three years later it was involved in Operation Granby, the British contribution to the US-led UN coalition forces which had been despatched to Saudi Arabia following the invasion and occupation of Kuwait by Iraq on 2 August 1990. This illegal move was followed by a lengthy game of diplomatic cat-and-mouse carried out by the UN Security Council and Iraq's leader, President Saddam Hussein, which culminated with the issue of Resolution 678. This gave the Iraqis until 15 January 1991 to pull out of Kuwait. At the same time armed forces were deployed in Saudi Arabia and the Gulf region in preparation for offensive operations to oust Iraqi forces from Kuwait. The battalion, under the command of Lieutenant-Colonel Seymour Monro, provided the headquarters and logistics echelon for the Armoured Delivery Group (ADG), a reserve force of equipment and 1,200 battlefield casualty replacements for the front line. Formed on 4 February 1991, the group consisted of three tank squadrons from the Life Guards, a squadron of armoured reconnaissance, three armoured infantry companies of the Scots Guards, a composite artillery battery and a composite engineer squadron.

At the same time the rest of the battalion was split up, with A Company providing the guard force for the headquarters of the British 1st Armoured Division while B Company carried out the same task for the headquarters of British Forces Middle East in Riyadh. Other Queen's Own Highlanders found themselves serving with 1st Royal Scots and 3rd Royal Regiment of Fusiliers (3RRF), but, as one of their number told the official historian of the war, it was an unsettling experience: 'when you go to war you want to be with the guys you worked with and trained with and lived with.' The ground attack began on 24 February and the coalition forces entered Kuwait four days later. During the operations three Queen's Own Highlanders were killed serving with 3RRF when two US A-10 'tank-buster' strike aircraft mistakenly opened fire on a column of British Warrior armoured fighting vehicles, killing nine British soldiers and wounding 11 others. They were replaced by Scots Guardsmen from ADG.

THE HIGHLANDERS (SEAFORTH, GORDONS AND CAMERONS)

At the end of the Gulf War 1st Queen's Own Highlanders returned to Münster prior to their eighth tour of duty in Northern Ireland. As it turned out, it would also be the regiment's final operational tour because another amalgamation was in the offing. In response to the end of the Cold War following the disintegration of the Soviet Union and the reunification of the two Germanys, the Conservative government produced its Defence White Paper, *Options for Change*, which proposed that the army should be reduced from 155,000 to 116,000 soldiers and that the infantry should lose 17 of its 55 battalions. In Scotland the regiments selected for amalgamation were The Royal Scots with The King's Own Scottish Borderers and Queen's Own Highlanders with The Gordon Highlanders. It was accepted that Scottish regiments would be affected but because most of the Scottish regiments had served in the Gulf the decision came as a shattering blow and immediate steps were taken to fight it. A well-organised and high-profile 'Keep Our Scottish Battalions' campaign was initiated under the chairmanship of Lieutenant-General Sir John Macmillan, a former GOC Scotland, and as a result the amalgamation of the two Lowland regiments was cancelled on 3 February 1993, together with the proposed amalgamation of the Cheshire and Staffordshire regiments.

However, the second Scottish amalgamation was ordered to proceed, even though it was only 32 years since the earlier amalgamation of The Seaforth and Cameron Highlanders. Following lengthy discussions between the two regiments it was agreed that the new regiment would be known as The Highlanders (Seaforth, Gordons and Camerons) and that its form of dress, traditions and battle honours would reflect the histories of the constituent regiments. As a result the new regiment retained the Queen's Own Highlanders' cap badge with the Seaforth motto

Cuidich 'n Righ, and to reflect the importance of the tartans all three were perpetuated in the new formation. All soldiers, less pipers and drummers, would wear the Gordon tartan kilt and a patch of Cameron tartan in the tam-o'-shanter bonnet; the pipers and drummers would wear the Cameron kilt with a patch of Gordon tartan in the bonnet; and the whole regiment would wear trews of Mackenzie tartan. In November 1993 1st Queen's Own Highlanders left Münster and moved into Dreghorn Barracks in Edinburgh in preparation for the amalgamation which was fixed for 17 September 1994. During the summer a number of farewell events took place, including a service of thanksgiving in the High Church of St Giles followed by a review of the regiment by the colonel-in-chief, HRH Prince Philip, Duke of Edinburgh. Three days before the amalgamation parade the two regular battalions took part in a ceremony on the bridge at Craigellachie on the River Spey, a picturesque and historic location which marks one of the boundaries of the two regimental areas.

Following the amalgamation 1st Battalion The Highlanders moved to Northern Ireland for a tour of duty, latterly in Londonderry, which ended in April 1997. Its next posting was to Somme Barracks in Catterick, Yorkshire, as part of 19 Mechanised Brigade. Between then and its return to Edinburgh in March 2001 the battalion supplied reinforcements for other infantry regiments serving in the Balkans (Bosnia and Kosovo) and carried out a six-month tour of duty in Armagh between June and December 2000. During this period the battalion was involved in two operations providing aid to the civil community – helping to co-ordinate measures to combat an outbreak of foot-and-mouth disease in 2002 and acting as emergency firefighters during the strike of 2003. In March 2004 the battalion moved to Fallingbostel in Germany to join 7 Armoured Brigade, and began training with the Warrior armoured fighting vehicle. Between November 2005 and May 2006 1ˢᵗ Highlanders served in Basra in southern Iraq as part of Britain's military commitment to the forces in the country following the operations to depose Saddam Hussein in 2003. Before the deployment, the regiment's future was already in doubt as a result of far-reaching reforms of the future structure of the infantry instigated by the Strategic Defence Review of July 2004. This time the change was even more radical, as it involved the reduction of the size of the infantry from 40 to 36 battalions, and that signalled the end for the remaining 19 single-battalion regiments. In their place large regiments consisting of several battalions were formed (a move that had begun in the 1960s); in Scotland this new formation was called The Royal Regiment of Scotland and The Highlanders formed its 4ᵗʰ battalion, serving as The Highlanders, 4ᵗʰ Battalion The Royal Regiment of Scotland. Formation day for the new regiment was 28 March 2006, while the battalion was still in Basra where one of its antecedents, 1ˢᵗ Seaforth, had served 90 years earlier. Although the moment was tinged with great sadness, that sense of history helped to create part of the 'golden thread' which binds the future of the new regiment to the past histories and glories of its constituent parts.

Appendix

REGIMENTAL FAMILY TREE
The Seaforth Highlanders
1st battalion (72nd)

1778: 78th (Highland) Regiment

1786: 72nd (Highland) Regiment

1804: 2nd battalion raised

1809: 72nd Foot

1816: 1st and 2nd battalions amalgamated

1823: 72nd (Duke of Albany's Own Highlanders)

1881: 1st battalion Seaforth Highlanders (Ross-shire Buffs)

1881: 1st battalion Seaforth Highlanders (Ross-shire Buffs, The Duke of Albany's)

1920: 1st battalion Seaforth Highlanders (Ross-shire Buffs, The Duke of Albany's)

1948: 1st and 2nd battalions amalgamated

2nd battalion

1793: 78th (Highland) Regiment

1794: 2nd battalion raised

1795: 78th (Highland) Regiment (Ross-shire Buffs)

1796: 1st and 2nd battalions amalgamated

1804: 2nd battalion re-raised

1817: 1st and 2nd battalions amalgamated

1881: 2nd battalion Seaforth Highlanders (Ross-shire Buffs)

1881: 2nd battalion Seaforth Highlanders (Ross-shire Buffs, The Duke of Albany's)

1920: 2nd battalion Seaforth Highlanders (Ross-shire Buffs, The Duke of Albany's)

1948: 1st and 2nd battalions amalgamated

Queen's Own Cameron Highlanders

1793: 79th Regiment (Cameronian Volunteers)

1804: 79th Regiment (Cameronian Highlanders)

1804: 2nd battalion raised

1806: 79th Cameron Highlanders

1815: 2nd battalion disbanded

1873: 79th Queen's Own Cameron Highlanders

1881: Queen's Own Cameron Highlanders

1897: 2nd battalion re-raised

1948: 1st and 2nd battalions amalgamated

1961: Queen's Own Highlanders (Seaforth and Camerons) following amalgamation of The Seaforth Highlanders with Queen's Own Cameron Highlanders

1994: The Highlanders (Seaforth, Gordons and Camerons) following amalgamation of Queen's Own Highlanders with The Gordon Highlanders

2006: The Highlanders, 4th battalion, The Royal Regiment of Scotland

REGIMENTAL BADGE

The badge of the Queen's Own Highlanders is officially described as 'A stag's head caboshed, between the attires of the Thistle, ensigned with the Crown, with the motto *Cuidich 'n Righ*.' The stag's head caboshed (showing no part of the neck) comes from the arms of the Mackenzie of Seaforth family and was used by the 72nd and 78th Highlanders. The badge of the 79th incorporated the figure of St Andrew and his cross and the Thistle and the Crown, the Badge of Scotland.

REGIMENTAL TARTANS

The two tartans associated with the regiment are the 78th or Mackenzie of Seaforth tartan, which was worn in the kilt, and the 79th or Cameron of Erracht tartan, which was worn in the kilt and plaid by the pipers, drummers and military bandsmen and as trews by the remainder of the regiment. In the first years the 78th wore government or Black Watch tartan on which the present tartan (with red and white stripes) is based, but the Cameron of Erracht tartan has the distinction of being the only regimental tartan which is not based on the government tartan. Between 1823 when it returned to Highland status and 1881, the 72nd wore Royal Stuart tartan with the Prince Charles Edward Stuart sett.

REGIMENTAL PIPE MUSIC

Pipers were not officially recognised by the army until 1854, when all Highland regiments were allowed a pipe-major and five pipers. Before that most Highland regiments employed pipers as a regimental expense and these were distributed throughout the regiment disguised on the muster roll as 'drummers'. The pipes and drums were always fully trained infantry soldiers and were in addition to the military band, which existed until 1994 when it was disbanded to form the Band of the Highland Division.

The regiment's pipe music is regularised as follows:

Regimental march past in quick time: Pibroch of Donuil Dubh

Regimental march: Cabar Feidh

Regimental march: The March of the Cameron Men

Regimental Slow March: The Garb of Old Gaul

Regimental Charge: The Standard on the Braes o' Mar

A Company: Dornoch Links

B Company: The Highland Brigade at Tel-el-Kebir

C Company: The Brown-haired Maiden

D Company: The Bugle Horn

S Company: The 51st Highland Division at Wadi Akarit

Headquarters Company: Over the Chindwin

BATTLE HONOURS

Two colours are carried by the regiment, the King's or Queen's, which is the Union flag, and the Regimental (originally First and Second Colour) which is buff with a Royal Blue fringe. In the centre, on a crimson background, is the regimental badge surrounded by the name of the regiment, and encircled by a wreath of thistles, roses and shamrocks, with the regimental motto *Cuidich 'n Righ* at the foot. The regimental colour also bears the following cyphers: the Cypher of HM Queen Victoria within the Garter; the Cypher and Coronet of HRH Prince Philip, Duke of Edinburgh; the Cypher and Coronet of HRH Prince Frederick Augustus, Duke of York; the Sphinx superscribed EGYPT, the battle honour awarded to the 79th Highlanders for the regiment's service in Egypt in 1801; an elephant superscribed ASSAYE, the battle honour awarded to the 78th Highlanders for the regiment's service at the Battle of Assaye in 1803.

During the Napoleonic Wars battle honours were added to the colours. In their final form, those gained during the First World War and the Second World War are carried on the Queen's

Colour and the remainder are carried on the Regimental Colour. At the outset battle honours were given sparingly or even randomly. In 1882 the system of battle honours was revised by a War Office committee under the chairmanship of General Sir Archibald Alison. It laid down guidelines whereby only victories would be included and most of the regiment had to be present. Additional refinements were made in 1907 and 1909 and their recommendations form the basis of the regiment's pre-1914 battle honours.

Pre-1914

Carnatic	Nivelle	Charasiah
Hindoostan	Nive	Kabul 1879
Mysore	Toulouse	Kandahar 1880
Egmont-op-Zee	Peninsula	Afghanistan 1878–80
Cape of Good Hope 1806	Waterloo	Tel-el-Kebir
	South Africa 1835	Egypt 1882
Maida	Alma	Nile 1884–85
Corunna	Sevastopol	Chitral
Busaco	Koosh-ab	Atbara
Fuentes d'Onor	Persia	Khartoum
Java	Lucknow	Paardeberg
Salamanca	Central India	South Africa
Pyrenees	Peiwar Kotal	1899–1902

The First World War

After the First World War there were further refinements to take cognisance of the size and complexity of the conflict. It was agreed that each regiment could carry ten major honours on their King's Colour but supporting operations would also receive battle honours which would not be displayed. The battle honours in bold type are carried on the Queen's Colour.

The Seaforth Highlanders and Queen's Own Cameron Highlanders (32 battalions)

Le Cateau

Retreat from Mons

Marne 1914, 1918

Aisne 1914

La Bassée 1914

Armentieres 1914

Ypres 1914, 1915, 1917, 1918

Langemarck 1914

Gheluvelt

Nonne Boschen

Festubert 1914, 1915

Givenchy 1914

Neuve Chapelle

Hill 60

Gravenstafel

St Julien

Frezenberg

Bellewaarde

Aubers

Loos

Somme 1916, 1918

Albert 1916

Bazentin

Delville Wood

Pozières

Flers-Courcelette

Morval

Le Transloy

Ancre Heights

Ancre 1916

Arras 1917, 1918

Vimy 1917

Scarpe 1917, 1918

Arleux

Pilckem

Menin Road

Polygon Wood

Broodseinde

Poelcapelle

Passchendaele

Cambrai 1917, 1918

St Quentin

Bapaume 1918

Lys

Estaires

Messines 1918

Hazebrouck

Bailleul

Kemmel

Bethunes

Soissonais-Ourcq

Tardenois

Drocourt-Queant

Hindenburg Line

Epehy

St Quentin Canal

Courtrai

Selle

Valenciennes

Sambre

France and Flanders 1914–18

Struma

Macedonia 1915–18

Megiddo

Sharon

Palestine 1918

Tigris 1916

Kut al Amara 1917

Baghdad

Mesopotamia 1915–18

The Second World War

In 1956 it was agreed to treat the Second World War in the same way. Those in bold type appear on the Queen's Colour.

The Seaforth Highlanders and Queen's Own Cameron Highlanders (10 battalions)

Defence of Escaut

St Omer-La Bassee

Ypres–Commines Canal

Somme 1940

Withdrawal to Seine

St Valéry-en-Caux

Odon

Cheux

Caen

Troarn

Mont Pinçon

Quarry Hill

Falaise

Falaise Road

Dives Crossing

La Vie Crossing

Lisieux

Nederrijn

Best

Le Havre

Lower Maas

Meijel

Venlo Pocket

Ourthe

Rhineland

Reichswald

Goch

Moyland

Rhine

Uelzen

Artlenburg

North-West Europe

1940, 1944–45

Agordat

Keren

Abyssinia 1941

Sidi Barrani

Tobruk 1941, 1942

Gubi II

Carmusa

Gazala

El Alamein

Advance on Tripoli

Mareth

Wadi Zigzaou

Akarit

Djebel Roumana

North Africa 1940–43

Landing in Sicily

Augusta

Francofonte

Adrano

Sferro Hills

Sicily 1943

Garigliano Crossing

Anzio

Cassiono I

Poggio del Grillo

Gothic Line

Tavoleto

Coriano

Pian di Castello

Monte Reggiano

Rimini Line

San Marino

Italy 1943–44

Madagascar

Middle East 1942

Imphal

Shenam Pass

Litan

Kohima

Relief of Kohima

Naga Village

Aradura

Tengnoupal

Shwebo

Mandalay

Ava

Irrawaddy

Mt Popa

Burma 1942–43

Post-1945

The battle honours gained since 1945 are carried on the Regimental Colour.

1ˢᵗ *Queen's Own Highlanders*
Gulf 1991

Allied and affiliated regiments
Canada

The Cameron Highlanders of Ottawa

Queen's Own Cameron Highlanders of Canada

The Seaforth Highlanders of Canada

Australia

10/27ᵗʰ Battalion The Royal South Australia Regiment

16ᵗʰ Battalion The Royal Western Australia Regiment

New Zealand

4ᵗʰ Battalion (Otago and Southland) The Royal New Zealand Infantry Regiment

7ᵗʰ Battalion Wellington (City of Wellington's Own) and Hawkes Bay The Royal New Zealand Infantry Regiment

7ᵗʰ Duke of Edinburgh's Own Gurkha Rifles (affiliation ceased in 1994 when the regiment became part of The Royal Gurkha Rifles)

WINNERS OF THE VICTORIA CROSS
Lieutenant A.C. Bogle, 78ᵗʰ Highlanders, Indian Mutiny, 1857

The regiment's first Victoria Cross was awarded to Lieutenant Andrew Cathcart Bogle, who led a party of soldiers into a position held by rebel sepoys at Oonao during the advance to Cawnpore. Despite coming under heavy fire he pressed home the attack and continued to display disciplined leadership even though he was badly wounded. A native of Glasgow, he died in Sherborne, Dorset, in 1890.

Lieutenant J.P.H. Crowe, 78th Highlanders, Indian Mutiny, 1857

South African-born Joseph Petrus Hendrick Crowe won his Victoria Cross under unusual circumstances. During an attack on rebel positions at Boorbia-Ki-Chauki in Oudh, Major-General Sir Henry Havelock promised that the first officer to enter a well-defended redoubt would be rewarded with the Victoria Cross. Two officers of the 78th Highlanders entered the position together – Lieutenants Crowe and Campbell – but the death of the latter from cholera settled the issue. Crowe eventually became a lieutenant-colonel and died in Penge, London, in 1876.

Lieutenant H.T. MacPherson, 78th Highlanders, Indian Mutiny, 1857

Herbert Taylor MacPherson was the adjutant of the 78th Highlanders when he was awarded the Victoria Cross during the operations to relieve Lucknow on 25 September 1857. A native of Ardersier in Inverness-shire, he led a charge on two artillery pieces which were threatening the regiment as it advanced along the Cawnpore road. Later, he was knighted and reached the rank of major-general. He died at Prome in Burma (now Myanmar) in 1886.

Surgeon Joseph Jee, 78th Highlanders, Indian Mutiny, 1857

A second Victoria Cross was won for the regiment at Lucknow by Surgeon Joseph Jee for his courage in tending to the wounded by leading them into the Residency while under heavy fire. Although exposed to heavy fire in the Mote Mehal he continued to dress the wounded and brought many of them to safety despite being warned not to make the attempt. He remained in the army to become deputy surgeon-general and died in 1899.

Assistant Surgeon Valentine McMaster, 78th Highlanders, Indian Mutiny, 1857

Following the courage shown by the 78th Highlanders during the operations to take the Residency in Lucknow it was decided to bestow the Victoria Cross on the entire regiment. The question was put to a vote by the men, who decided that the recipient should be McMaster, who continually exposed himself to hostile fire whilst bringing in the wounded. Born in India in 1834, McMaster died in Belfast in 1872.

Colour Sergeant Stewart McPherson, 78th Highlanders, Indian Mutiny, 1857

According to the entry in the *London Gazette* of 12 April 1859, Stewart McPherson, a native of Culross in Fife, was awarded the Victoria Cross 'For daring gallantry in the Lucknow Residency on 26 September 1857, in having rescued at great personal risk a wounded private of his company who was lying in a most exposed position under very heavy fire. Colour Sergeant McPherson was also distinguished on many occasions by his coolness and gallantry in action.' He died in 1892.

Private Henry Ward, 78th Highlanders, Indian Mutiny, 1857

While escorting a badly wounded officer, Captain Havelock 10th Foot, under heavy fire, Ward prevented the Indian bearers from running off after another wounded private soldier joined the party. Showing the same steadiness as if on parade, Ward's example inspired the bearers to bring the wounded men to safety. Later Ward became

Havelock's soldier-servant and reached the rank of quartermaster sergeant. He died ten years later in Malvern, Worcestershire.

Private James Hollowell, 78th Highlanders, Indian Mutiny, 1857

During the operations to take the Residency in Lucknow Hollowell (also Holliwell) was left behind with a party of wounded along with Surgeon A.D. Home, 90th Light Infantry, who was also awarded the Victoria Cross. Under fierce fire they fought their way into a nearby house and relative safety. When it was set ablaze they retreated into a shed where Hollowell led a successful defence before being rescued. He died in London in 1876.

Lieutenant A.S. Cameron, 72nd Highlanders, Indian Mutiny, 1858

During the operations against the Rani of Jhansi in south India Aylmer Spicer Cameron led an attack on a strongly defended building at Kotah and killed three of the rebels single-handedly. Although the attack was successful Cameron had half a hand chopped off but remained in the army. He reached the rank of colonel and died at Alverstock in Hampshire in 1909.

Lance-Corporal George Sellar, 72nd Highlanders, Afghanistan, 1879

During an attack on Afghan positions on the Asmai Heights outside Kabul on 14 December 1879 George Sellar dashed ahead of his group and engaged in hand-to-hand fighting with the enemy. Despite being wounded he pressed home his attack and the position was taken. Over 600 Afghans died during the assault by the British field force. A native of Keith, Sellar died at Lairg in Sutherland in 1889.

Sergeant John Mackenzie, 2nd Seaforth Highlanders, Doompassi, Ashanti, 1900

While serving with the West African Frontier Force in the Third Ashanti Expedition of 1900–01, led by Brigadier-General James Willcocks, John Mackenzie was awarded the Victoria Cross at Doompassi. Although he was wounded he continued to direct the fire of two Maxim guns and cleared the enemy from the stockades at bayonet point. He was later commissioned and was killed in action at Bethune in May 1915.

Sergeant Donald Farmer, 1st Cameron Highlanders, Boer War, 1900

The first Victoria Cross to be awarded to a Cameron Highlander was won by Donald Farmer of the Mounted Infantry company, a native of Kelso. At Nooitgedacht he was part of a small force that went to the assistance of a picquet that had been attacked by a Boer column. When the senior officer, Lieutenant Sandilands, was wounded Farmer carried him to safety before returning to the firing line, where he was taken prisoner. Later he was commissioned. He died in Liverpool in 1956.

Private Ross Tollerton, 1st Cameron Highlanders, First World War, 1914

During the Battle of the Aisne Tollerton carried Lieutenant J.S.M. Matheson to safety before returning to the firing line. Although wounded himself, he returned to Matheson's side when the battalion retired and stayed with him for three days before both men were rescued. He died in Irvine in 1931.

Lieutenant-Colonel A.F. Douglas-Hamilton, 6th Cameron Highlanders, First World War, 1915

Battalion commanders were awarded the Victoria Cross only

under exceptional circumstances and Sussex-born Angus Falconer Douglas-Hamilton was awarded his posthumously for his leadership and courage under fire at Hill 70 during the Battle of Loos. Again and again he rallied his men under heavy fire and, according to the citation in the *London Gazette*, 'it was mainly due to his bravery, untiring energy and splendid leadership that the line at this point was enabled to check the enemy's advance'.

Corporal James D. Pollock, 5th Cameron Highlanders, First World War, 1915

During the fighting on the Hohenzollern Redoubt during the Battle of Loos James Dalgleish Pollock got out of his trench alone to throw grenades into a German position, forcing them to retire. Throughout his single-handed attack he exposed himself to heavy fire and showed a complete disregard for his own safety. He survived the war and died in Ayr in 1958.

Corporal Sidney Ware, 1st Seaforth Highlanders, First World War, 1916

A native of Whatcombe in Devon, Sidney Ware was awarded the Victoria Cross during the operations at Sannaiyat in Mesopotamia on 6 April 1916. During a withdrawal he carried one wounded man to safety and returned to help others while under heavy enemy fire. All were eventually rescued but Ware died ten days later from his wounds.

Drummer Walter Ritchie, 2nd Seaforth Highlanders, First World War, 1916

On the first day of the Battle of the Somme Drummer Walter Ritchie from Glasgow was one of nine soldiers to be awarded the Victoria Cross. Acting on his own initiative he rallied the men by standing on the parapet of an enemy position and sounding the

'Charge'. Throughout the rest of the day he continued to act as a messenger over fire-swept ground. He survived the war and died in Edinburgh in 1965.

Sergeant Thomas Steele, 1st Seaforth Highlanders, First World War, 1917

Awarded during the campaign against Ottoman forces in Mesopotamia during an attack on enemy positions at Sannaiyat. At a critical moment during a Turkish counter-attack Steele rushed forward, brought a machine-gun into action and kept firing until relieved. Some hours later he rallied wavering troops and despite being wounded led a spirited counter-attack. A native of Lancashire, he died in Oldham in 1978.

Lieutenant Donald Mackintosh, 2nd Seaforth Highlanders, First World War, 1917

Although this young officer was shot in the leg during an attack on German positions near Fampoux he led his men into an enemy trench and held it against counter-attack. With 15 remaining men under his command he led a fresh attack and was killed during the course of the action. A native of Glasgow, Mackintosh was only 21.

Sergeant Alexander Edwards, 6th Seaforth Highlanders, First World War, 1917

Summarising the courage and leadership qualities shown by Alexander Edwards during the Third Battle of Ypres, when he led an attack on a German machine-gun position, the *London Gazette* recorded: 'Although twice wounded ... this very gallant Non-commissioned Officer maintained throughout a complete disregard for his personal safety and his high example of coolness and determination engendered a fine fighting spirit amongst his men.' A native of Lossiemouth, Edwards was killed in action at Bapaume the following year.

Lance-Corporal Robert McBeath, 5ᵗʰ Seaforth Highlanders, First World War, 1917

When his company's attack was checked during the Battle of Cambrai, McBeath went ahead alone with a Lewis gun and attacked the enemy position with the support of a tank. He succeeded in capturing the German trench and took prisoner over 30 soldiers. After the war McBeath, a native of Kinlochbervie, emigrated to Canada where he joined the police. He was killed in a shoot-out in Vancouver in 1922.

Sergeant John Meikle, 4ᵗʰ Seaforth Highlanders, First World War, 1918

While fighting in the Ardre Valley during the Battle of the Marne in the summer of 1918 John Meikle attacked a German position single-handedly and succeeded in putting two machine-guns out of action. When another machine-gun position opened fire he again rushed forward to try to silence it but was killed during the attack. A native of Nitshill in Renfrewshire, he had previously been awarded the Military Medal.

Bibliography

Unless otherwise stated, extracts from soldiers' letters and diaries are in the possession of the regiment or are housed in the Imperial War Museum or the National Army Museum, London. Quotations from battalion and brigade War Diaries or other official papers are housed in the National Archives, Kew.

Books about The Seaforth Highlanders, Queen's Own Cameron Highlanders and Queen's Own Highlanders (Seaforth and Camerons)

Addison-Smith, Lieutenant-Colonel C.L., *10ʰᵗ Battalion Seaforth Highlanders in the Great War*, J. Bain & Sons, Edinburgh, 1927

Baynes, Captain Kenneth S., *Narrative of the part played by the 79ᵗʰ Queen's Own Cameron Highlanders in the Egyptian Campaign*, Henry Hansard & Son, London, 1883

Borthwick, Alastair, *Sans Peur: 5ᵗʰ Battalion Seaforth Highlanders in World War II*, Eneas Mackay, Stirling, 1946

Cameron, Major N. J.G., *South African War Record of the 1ˢᵗ Battalion The Queen's Own Cameron Highlanders*, Northern Counties Printing, Elgin, 1903

Cannon, Richard, *Historical Records of the 72nd Regiment*, Furnival & Parker, London, 1848

Davidson, Major Hugh, *History and Services of the 78th Highlanders*, 2 vols, W. & A.K. Johnston, Edinburgh, 1901; (ed.), *The Seaforth Highlanders in South Africa 1899–02*, W. & A.K. Johnston, Edinburgh, 1904

Egerton, Major-General Granville, *With the Seaforth Highlanders in the Sudan Campaign*, Eden Fisher & Co., London, 1909

Fairrie, Lieutenant-Colonel Angus, *Queen's Own Highlanders (Seaforth and Camerons)*, Northern Times, Golspie, 1998 (2nd revised edition of *Cuidich 'n Righ: A History of the Queen's Own Highlanders*, Northern Times, Golspie, 1983)

Groves, Lieutenant-Colonel Percy, *History of the 79th Queen's Own Cameron Highlanders, now the 1st Battalion Queen's Own Cameron Highlanders 1794–1893*, W. & A.K. Johnston, Edinburgh and London, 1893

Haldane, Lieutenant-Colonel M.M., *A History of the 4th Battalion Seaforth Highlanders*, H.T. & G. Witherby, London, 1927

Historical Records Committee, *Historical Records of the Cameron Highlanders*, 7 vols, William Blackwood, Edinburgh, 1909–62

Jackson, John, *Private 12768: Memoir of a Tommy*, Tempus, Stroud, 2004

Jameson, Captain Robert, *Historical Records of the 79th Regiment or Cameron Highlanders*, William Blackwood, Edinburgh, 1863

Mackenzie, Captain T.A., Ewart, Lieutenant J.S., and Findlay, Lieutenant C., *Historical Records of the 79th Queen's Own Cameron Highlanders*, Hamilton Adams & Co., London, 1887

Mackintosh, Ewart Alan, *A Highland Regiment*, John Lane, London, 1917; *War, the Liberator*, John Lane, London, 1918

Maclean of Dochgarroch, Lorraine, *The Raising of the 79th Highlanders*, Society of West Highland & Island Historical Research, Inverness, 1980; *Indomitable Colonel: The Biography of Lieutenant-Colonel Sir Alan Cameron of Erracht*, Shepheard-Walwyn, London, 1986

BIBLIOGRAPHY

MacLeod, Lieutenant-Colonel Norman, *War History of the 6th (Service) Battalion The Queen's Own Cameron Highlanders*, William Blackwood, Edinburgh, 1934

MacVeigh, James, *Historical Records of the 78th Highlanders*, J. Maxwell & Sons, Dumfries, 1887; *Historical Records of the 79th Highlanders*, J. Maxwell & Sons, Dumfries, 1888

Melville, Major Michael Leslie, *The Story of the Lovat Scouts 1900–80*, St Andrew Press, Edinburgh, 1981

Sandilands, Colonel J.W., and MacLeod, Lieutenant-Colonel Norman, *History of the 7th (Service) Battalion The Queen's Own Cameron Highlanders*, Eneas Mackay, Stirling, 1922

Stockman, Jim, *Seaforth Highlanders: A Fighting Soldier Remembers*, Crecy Books, Somerton, 1987

Sutherland, Captain David, *War Diary of the 5th Battalion Seaforth Highlanders*, John Lane, London, 1920

Sym, Colonel John, *Seaforth Highlanders*, Gale & Polden, Aldershot, 1962

Todd, Andrew, *The Elephant at War: The 2nd Battalion Seaforth Highlanders*, The Pentland Press, Bishop Auckland, 1998

Other books consulted

Ascoli, David, *A Companion to the British Army 1660–1983*, Harrap, London, 1983

Barnett, Correlli, *Britain and her Army 1509–70*, Allen Lane, London, 1970; *The Lost Victory: British Dreams, British Realities 1945–50*, Macmillan, London, 1995

Baynes, John, with Laffin, John, *Soldiers of Scotland*, Brassey's, London, 1988

Bewsher, F.W., *The History of the 51st (Highland) Division 1914–18*, William Blackwood, Edinburgh, 1921

Brereton, J.M., *The British Army: A Social History of the British Army from 1661 to the Present Day*, The Bodley Head, London, 1986

Chandler, David, and Beckett, Ian (eds.), *The Oxford Illustrated History of the British Army*, Oxford University Press, Oxford, 1994

David, Saul, *Churchill's Sacrifice of the Highland Division*, Brassey's, London, 1994; *The Indian Mutiny 1857*, Viking, London, 2002

Delaforce, Patrick, *Monty's Highlanders, 51ˢᵗ Highland Division in World War Two*, Tom Donovan, Brighton, 1997

Duff, James Grant, *A History of the Mahrattas*, 3 vols, Longmans, London, 1826

Ewing, John, *History of the 9ᵗʰ (Scottish) Division 1914–19*, John Murray, London, 1921

Fitchett, W.H., *The Tale of the Great Mutiny*, Smith Elder, London, 1899

Fortescue, Sir John, *A History of the British Army*, 13 vols, Macmillan, London, 1899–30

Hamley, E.B., *The Operations of War Explained and Illustrated*, William Blackwood, Edinburgh, 1878

Henderson, Diane, *The Scottish Regiments*, Collins, Glasgow, 1996

Hingston, W.G., *The Tiger Strikes: History of the 4ᵗʰ Indian Division*, Thackers Press, Calcutta, 1942

Holmes, Richard (ed.), *The Oxford Companion to Military History*, Oxford University Press, Oxford, 2001

Jackson, Bill and Bramall, Dwin, *The Chiefs: The Story of the United Kingdom Chiefs of Staff*, Brassey's, London, 1992

Keay, John, *The Honourable Company: A History of the East India Company*, HarperCollins, London, 1991

Keegan, John, *Six Armies in Normandy*, Jonathan Cape, London, 1982

Kinglake, A.W., *The Invasion of the Crimea*, 8 vols, William Blackwood, Edinburgh, 1863–87

Linklater, Eric, *The Highland Division*, HMSO, London, 1942; *The Campaign in Italy*, HMSO, London, 1951

BIBLIOGRAPHY

Mileham, P. J.R., *Scottish Regiments*, Spellmount, Tunbridge Wells, 1988

Neillands, Robin, *A Fighting Retreat: The British Empire 1947–97*, Hodder & Stoughton, London, 1996

Pearce, Nigel, *The Shield and the Sabre: The Desert Rats in the Gulf 1990–91*, HMSO, London, 1992

Prebble, John, *Mutiny: Highland Regiments in Revolt*, Secker & Warburg, London, 1975

Royle, Trevor, *The Best Years of Their Lives: The National Service Experience 1945–1963*, Michael Joseph, London, 1986; *Crimea: The Great Crimean War 1854–1856*, Little Brown, London, 1999

Salmond, J.B., *The History of the 51ˢᵗ Highland Division 1939–45*, William Blackwood, Edinburgh, 1953

Sterling, Anthony, *The Story of the Highland Brigade in the Crimea*, Absinthe Press, Minneapolis, 1995 (originally published 1895)

Stewart of Garth, David, *Sketches of the Character, Manners and present State of the Highlanders of Scotland, with details of the Military Service of the Highland Regiments*, 2 vols, Constable, Edinburgh, 1822

Stewart, J. and Buchan, John, *The 15ᵗʰ (Scottish) Division 1914–19*, William Blackwood, Edinburgh, 1926

Strawson, John, *Gentlemen in Khaki: The British Army 1890–90*, Hutchinson, London, 1989; *Beggars in Red: The British Army 1789–1889*, Hutchinson, London, 1991

Wood, Stephen, *The Scottish Soldier*, Archive Publications, Manchester, 1987

INDEX

INDEX